TESTIMONIES OF FAITH AND ENCOURAGEMENT

A WEEKLY DEVOTIONAL
BY BILLY JACKSON OF LIVE IN PEACE PUBLISHING

TESTIMONIES OF FAITH AND ENCOURAGEMENT

A WEEKLY DEVOTIONAL
BY BILLY JACKSON OF LIVE IN PEACE PUBLISHING
NASHVILLE

Testimonies of Encouragement and Faith: A Weekly Devotional
© 2021 by Billy Jackson
All Rights Reserved
Published by Live in Peace Ministries, LLC
P.O. Box 2772
Nashville, TN 37077

No part of this book may be reproduced or transmitted in any form or by any means, electronic or mechanical, including photocopying, recording, or any information storage retrieval system without prior permission in writing from the publisher.

Queries regarding rights and permissions should be addressed to:
Live in Peace Ministries, LLC
P.O. Box 2772, Nashville, TN 37077
www.liveinpeaceministries.org

Manufactured in the United States of America

Interior design by: Arlana Johnson

Cover Design by: The Grace Effect

ISBN: 978-0-578-89713-4

Scripture quotations taken identified by NKJV are taken from the New King James Version® Copyright 1982 by Thomas Nelson. Used by permission. All rights reserved.

Scripture quotations marked (NIV) are taken from The Holy Bible, New International Version® NIV® Copyright © 1973 1978 1984 2011 by Biblica, Inc. ™ Used by permission. All rights reserved worldwide.

Scripture quotations marked (NIRV) are taken from the Holy Bible, NEW INTERNATIONAL READER'S VERSION®. Copyright © 1996, 1998 Biblica. All rights reserved throughout the world. Used by permission of Biblica.

Scripture quotations marked (NLT) are taken from the Holy Bible, New Living Translation, copyright ©1996, 2004, 2015 by Tyndale House Foundation. Used by permission of Tyndale House Publishers, Carol Stream, Illinois 60188. All rights reserved.

Scripture quotations marked CSB and HCSB have been taken from the Christian Standard Bible®, Copyright 2017 by Holman Bible Publishers. Used by permission. Christian Standard Bible® and CSB® are federally registered trademarks of Holman Bible Publishers.

Scripture quotations marked MSG are taken from THE MESSAGE, copyright © 1993, 2002, 2018 by Eugene H. Peterson. Used by permission of NavPress. All rights reserved. Represented by Tyndale House Publishers, Inc.

Scripture quotation Psalm 19:14 is from the ESV ® Bible (The Holy Bible, English Standard Version®), copyright ©2001 by Crossway, a publishing ministry of Good News Publishers. Used by permission. All rights reserved.

DEDICATION

I dedicate this work of the Lord written by and through me, to my wife Yolanda. There are many reasons why she is at the center of this devotional, but most importantly, she is my foundation, and her actions gave birth to our ministry, Live in Peace. No matter the challenges we've faced in our marriage, Yolanda never gave in to her desire to quit and count us out, even when my actions drained her of her peace.

She was the first of us to submit to the Lord and allow His will, not only for her life, but for the strength and healing of our marriage. It is because of this love from her heart of God and of His will for our marriage, that I was able to produce these writings. Because of her, God revealed Himself to me, a lost soul caught in a powerful grip of addiction, anger, and selfishness—a revelation I would never have seen had Yolanda not prayed, carried her burdens to the cross and believed that God was bigger than what was holding us back.

This work, created from spirit to spirit, is dedicated solely to my beautiful wife of 14 years. Thank you, Yolanda. I love you.

CONTENTS

Acknowledgments	xiii
Introduction	xiv
Week One: Rejoice in God's Plans for You in the New Year	1
Week Two: Train Your Palate to a New Taste	3
Week Three: Allow God's Seed to Grow Within You	5
Week Four: Examine Yourself, and Exercise Your Faith	7
Week Five: Tap into the Power Within You	9
Week Six: Cast Off Your Feelings of Unworthiness	11
Week Seven: God Has a Plan for You	13
Week Eight: Accept God's Gift of Faith	15
Week Nine: As We Are Comforted, Let Us to Be of Comfort	17
Week Ten: Discipline Your Flesh in the Word	19
Week Eleven: Curb the Power of the Tongue	21
Week Twelve: Seeing "The Horse in the Stone"	23
Week Thirteen: Accept Your Blessing and Be Healed	25
Week Fourteen: Sing God's Praises	27
Week Fifteen: The Lesson of the Fiery Furnace	29
Week Sixteen: Be Patient Through Your Trials	31
Week Seventeen: Show Others the God in You	33

Week Eighteen: Obey the Father's Commandments 35

Week Nineteen: We Are Transformed by Our Suffering 37

Week Twenty: You Are a Star 39

Week Twenty-One: Remain the Soldier 41

Week Twenty-Two: Be a Conduit for God's Blessings 43

Week Twenty-Three: Let Go of Your Mind-set of Sin 45

Week Twenty-Four: Let God Act on Your Behalf 47

Week Twenty-Five: Let Us Love Through Action and Truth 49

Week Twenty-Six: You Are Protected 51

Week Twenty-Seven: Cast Aside Unworthiness 53

Week Twenty-Eight: Come to Know God 55

Week Twenty-Nine: Always Pray with Enthusiasm 57

Week Thirty: Allow God to Do His Best with Your Worst 59

Week Thirty-One: The Lifeguard with Us 61

Week Thirty-Two: Supplement Your Faith With Goodness 63

Week Thirty-Three: Pray for Wisdom Through God's Word 65

Week Thirty-Four: Pray for the Protection of Others 67

Week Thirty-Five: Remember What God Has Done for You 69

Week Thirty-Six: Condition Yourself Through Spring Training 71

Week Thirty-Seven: Rely on Godly Weapons to Defeat the Enemy 73

Week Thirty-Eight: Resist Temptation: Arm Yourself with the Word 75

Week Thirty-Nine: Change Your Attitude, and Follow God's Will 77

Week Forty: The Importance of Instruction	79
Week Forty-One: Discipline Your Flesh to Live by the Spirit	81
Week Forty-Two: Purify Yourself: Be Who God Created You to Be	83
Week Forty-Three: Endure Through Your Suffering	85
Week Forty-Four: Accept God's Cover in Good Times and Bad	87
Week Forty-Five: Renew Your Inner Self Every Day	89
Week Forty-Six: Your Testimony Is Your Strength	91
Week Forty-Seven: The Treasures You Hold in Your Heart	93
Week Forty-Eight: Be Transformed by the Spirit	95
Week Forty-Nine: Wait for the Lord. Put Your Trust in Him	97
Week Fifty: Risk Being a Disciple, No Matter the Cost	99
Week Fifty-One: God's Promises to the Faithful	101
Week Fifty-Two: Claim the Strength to Move Mountains	103
Scriptures for Further Reading	105
Final Prayer to the Holy Spirit	109
About the Author	111

ACKNOWLEDGMENTS

I would like to first thank God for giving me the wisdom of His Word and guidance to direct His power to those who have prayed for His healing and strength.

I would like to recognize and thank my pastor and father-in-law, the Reverend William R. Harris, Sr. It is through him that my spiritual journey began. For the first time in my life, I was going to church every Sunday again, attending the church he pastored. Eventually I became a deacon, and after transformation and much study, Pastor Harris ordained me as I became one of his associate ministers. Reverend Harris is one of the foundations in my being grounded in a strong relationship with Jesus Christ.

I would also like to recognize Dr. Mark McPherson, President of the Emmanuel Bible College, and Dr. Debbie Thomas, both of whom gave me the chance to study the Word of God and earn a degree at Emmanuel Bible College. Through their incredible institution I was able to not only earn a degree, but also gain the wisdom needed to keep my relationship with God strong.

I would like to sincerely thank my editor, Mr. Mark Boone. I bring him a stone that I think is valuable, and he guides me in chipping away here and polishing it there until the result is the most beautiful piece of writing it can be.

May God continue to bless all of you in blessing others, the way you have blessed me.

INTRODUCTION

The inspiration for these devotions came from a retreat that my wife Yolanda and I hosted under the auspices of Live in Peace Ministries. We began this journey of hosting retreats in 2016. One particular session of the retreat schedule enabled the wives to spend some time with Yolanda, and the husbands to spend time with me. As I spoke to the husbands, many of them said that in their busy schedules and within their comfort zones they could not find the time to devote to God's Word on a daily basis.

I shared my personal story of transformation from a man in the grip of an addiction to alcohol, to one who submitted to God's healing hand and became freed by His Living Word. I told them how becoming immersed in the Living Word could become a habit and a means of salvation for them too, if they give it the chance.

Then, the Lord placed in my spirit a way to stay in contact with these men and assist them in forming a relationship with the Lord by spending more time in His Word. God allowed me to share the gift of His message through the devotionals that you will find in this book.

Beginning in the Fall of 2017, I began writing them and sending them out every Wednesday to a list of spiritually hungry husbands from our retreat groups. The list has grown since then and now is shared with and read by women also. It is because of its impact on those who receive it that the Holy Spirit has led me to make it available for all whom God intends to be touched by these testimonies.

These devotions are scripturally based, and most are coupled with transparent testimonies related to different situations that have arisen in my life that God has brought me through. They are written with the goal of building the habit of giving God His time every day through reading and meditating on His Word. It is my prayer that this book will enable the believer to grow closer to God and get to know Him as He intends and wants us to.

This book is arranged into fifty-two devotionals (one devotional a week), for a year's worth of spiritual habit-forming time with God. It is my hope that you begin the week with each one, reflect on its message and the scriptures related to it, apply it to your own circumstances, and thereby deepen your relationship with God.

At the end of the book are additional scriptures for you to meditate upon, chosen specifically for the relevance to the theme of the particular week. Once you have read and prayed over the devotion, I encourage you to refer to these scriptures to help build your daily habit of spending time with God.

I pray that this book, with God's power and guidance, will help you to overcome your bad habits and form new godly, healthier habits that keep your mind, body, and soul focused on the Most High.

WEEK ONE
Rejoice in God's Plans for You in the New Year

"For I know the plans I have for you"—this is the Lord's declaration—
"plans for your well-being, not disaster, to give you a future and a hope."
Jeremiah 29:11 ~CSB

As we ring in the New Year, let the love of God come into your heart as well. A love that knows God's intentions for you. God created you for a purpose and with that purpose, blessings especially made for you will come!

So, starting this year, don't let the devil lie to you any longer! Don't let him tell you that what you are going through is normal. It's all a lie. Don't let the devil tell you that you've reaped all you are going to reap in this life. It's a lie. Don't let him tell you that joy is only a figment of your imagination and will never exist in your heart. It's a lie.

God is telling you that He has plans for you! He declared it in Jeremiah 29:11! These plans are not what the devil is whispering in your ear. No. God's plans are for your well-being, not the times you are going through. God has already laid out a future of hope for you! All you have to do is trust, believe, and receive what God has planned and completed for you!

Remember, God did not sacrifice His One and Only Son so that you can live a life without blessing. As He created the heavens and earth with such magnificent power and artistry, so did He create you; and it was not so that you could fall short. In this New Year declare blessings on your:

- Life
- Relationships
- Marriage

- Children
- Finances
- Health
- And your relationship with God!!!

Believe and receive God's love and gift of an abundant life as you pray in thanksgiving for everything He has done, is doing and will do in your life!

So praise God on this day, in this new year, for His saving grace and mercy in Jesus' name.

Amen.

WEEK TWO
Train Your Palate to a New Taste

"Blessed are those who hunger and thirst for righteousness, For they shall be filled." Matthew 5:6 ~NKJV

From 1990 to 2013 my blood pressure always registered high. In 1993, I was almost denied entry into the Armed Forces because of the condition. When my son Will was born in 2008, the Holy Spirit spoke to my heart about taking better care of myself.

I've always worked out and taken care of my external appearance, but I had neglected my body's internal workings. I now had to learn what was good for my body and what was detrimental to it: what was digestible and healthy as opposed to what was indigestible and toxic. I had to learn to reduce the sodium content of my food, forgo a diet of pork, and eliminate foods cooked in fat from my diet. All the things that made food taste good to me at the time I had to let go of.

The Bible says in 1 Corinthians 10:23: *"…I am allowed to do anything but not everything is good for you…I am allowed to do anything but not everything is beneficial…"* ~NLT

Upon reading this scripture I realized that what might taste good to me may not be good for me, which meant researching foods that were good for me, regardless of how they tasted.

Let's take this same concept and apply it to God's Word in our lives. The world would have us to live an ungodly lifestyle, think ungodly thoughts, and act in ungodly ways. We have the capacity to lie and deceive, to be selfish and abusive. Our tendency to show anger, commit sexual sins, impure acts, and wild living can be strong. Add to it a palate trained to tolerate hatred, fighting, and jealousy, and you have a toxic diet that will lead to certain death.

But if we train our palates for a new taste, we can improve our spiritual health. No matter what the world has shown us, we will seek what is good. For James 1:17 says, *"Every good and perfect gift is from God."* ~NIRV

We then begin to seek the good in God's Word, a Word that can teach us to become kind and forgiving. To love, have joy in our hearts, and find peace in the midst of our struggles. As we grow in God's Word, we begin to hunger for more of His love. And when we thirst for Him, He will fill us. This new healthy diet born of our acclimation to a "new taste" feeds our spirit, and when the Holy Spirit within us grows strong, it helps us fight the desires of the flesh. And everything else in us that is ungodly.

Righteousness then becomes digestible in the temple God has created for us, and it is the fruit that allows us to live godly lives. So, train your taste for what's good, which comes from God.

May He continue to cover you, guide you, and grant you the wisdom you need in Jesus' name.

Amen.

WEEK THREE
Allow God's Seed to Grow Within You

"The seed that fell among thorns stands for those who hear the message. But as they go on their way, they are choked by life's worries, riches, and pleasures. So they do not reach full growth." Luke 8:14 ~NIRV

During church, most of us feel the hope and the love of God in our hearts as we sing praises to His name and hear the Word God sends to us through His messenger. We take our trials and tribulations to the altar and thank God for taking our burdens from us. We might even shed a tear because we are so happy, and for the first time that week, feel as though a weight has been lifted off us! After service, in genuine love, we hug each other with the words, "Bless you brother!" or "May God keep you, sister, until we meet again!"

We may not even get out of the parking lot before the world waylays us, stirring our flesh, deflating our spirit. The Word that we just heard, turns into a pipedream as life shows its face and makes us bow to it. It might be an unexpected phone call; it could be traffic; it could be the reminder that your rent is due Tuesday, and you don't have the money to pay it.

The seeds from the Word you heard minutes earlier have not taken root. They "fell among thorns…" The message was "heard," but what was heard was not "received."

When a fullback runs holding the ball with one hand, a defensive player can easily come along and knock it out of his hand, exactly what happens when we merely hear the Word and don't receive it. The world knocks the Word right out of us, or otherwise takes it away from us so that we remain in bondage.

But like the fullback who tucks the ball into him, ducks his head, and runs through the defense, so must we as Christians do having received the Word of God. We must hold on to it with all our might, so that whatever situation we are faced with, we can run through it without ever losing our grip!

Sure, we might fall from time to time, but we must still hang on to the Word as we get back up and continue our journey forward with God's Word inside us.

As the text continues in Luke 8: Verse 15: *"But the seed on good soil stands for those with an honest and good heart. Those people hear the message. They keep it in their hearts. They remain faithful and produce a good crop."* ~NIRV

Remain faithful and know that God's Word contains His promise. When that seed grows within, you will be directed to the promise God has for you.

May He give you the strength, wisdom, and direction you need on your journey in Jesus' name.

Amen.

WEEK FOUR
Examine Yourself, and Exercise Your Faith

"Therefore, whoever eats the bread or drinks the cup of the Lord in an unworthy way will be guilty of sin against the body and blood of the Lord. So a man should examine himself; in this way he should eat the bread and drink from the cup." 1 Corinthians 11:27-28 ~HCSB

When I was a boy, we would recite the pledge of allegiance at school all the time, and at that time in my life, all it meant to me was that it was something we recited every morning during announcements. It was something I learned to say in my sleep.

In 1993 when I joined the United States Army, the pledge became transformed into a covenant with the country in which I was born and raised. A nation that I would take an oath to protect. It thus became the pledge that it was meant to be. From that day on I would always be conscious of what I spoke into existence and of what I stood for.

As Christians, we must know and live by our covenant with God and His covenant with us. The covenant that God had with Abraham is the same covenant God has with us. And this covenant comes as a result of the sacrifice of His Son, Jesus.

As Christians we must live a life dedicated to getting to know Jesus as our Lord and Savior. We must do this because the world has conformed us to its limits and shortcomings and has taught us to rely solely on its existence. Our flesh is weak, and like a magnet, the world pulls at us every day, keeping us from realizing the potential of our victory in God because our spirit lacks the strength to overcome the world's pull.

Our spirit needs a workout that can only come from exercising our faith. Our faith is tested every day: "Will I be able to pay my rent? Will I get my car fixed so I can get back and forth to work? Will I be able to fight this cancer diagnosis?"

When we pass these tests, our questions cease to exist, and our declarations of victory become more frequent. It doesn't matter what the doctor says, by His stripes I am healed! I know the Lord will keep a roof over my head because He loves me, and I work hard for Him every day!

2 Corinthians 13:5 says, *"Test yourselves to see if you are in the faith. Examine yourselves. Or do you yourselves not recognize that Jesus Christ is in you? —unless you fail the test."* ~HCSB

Don't fall short. Don't find yourself lacking by failing the test of faith. Don't find yourselves wanting because you do not realize that Christ is in you.

God loves you and wants the best for you. Take the knowledge of His Son and always know that this is the "good seed" of faith in all who love the Lord.

May God continue to bless and keep you on your journey in Jesus' name.

Amen.

WEEK FIVE
Tap into the Power Within You

"Therefore, My Father loves Me, because I lay down My life that I may take again. 18 No one takes it from Me, but I lay it down of Myself. I have power to lay it down, and I have power to take it again. This command I have received from My Father." John 10:17-18 ~NKJV

Jesus Christ said His life was His to give. He said His life was also His to take back. It was given to lay down our sins and was taken back for our salvation—the blueprint for the promised eternal life! Let's pause and give God a shout of praise!

I learned this power firsthand by what Jesus did for my transformation. There I was, at least twenty-three years in a grip of an alcoholism so strong that I could not break free from it. I wanted it more than I wanted my family. Under its influence, I lied to and deceived my wife. I was so blind to God's will and purpose for my life that I was on the brink of losing everything.

A tragic accident, in the midst of my submission to the Word of God in my heart led to my old weak flesh being buried and myself being created anew! By the hand of God, the poison of alcohol addiction was taken from me, and I craved it no more!

Jesus says to us in John 10:27 that [He will] *"…give them eternal life, and they shall never perish; neither shall anyone snatch them out of My hand."* ~NKJV

We were given to Him by the Father! Being chosen is something to shout about! Being chosen means that no matter what we are going through, the enemy cannot claim us. So whatever situation you are in, the enemy can't win! The reason why trials appear to be so tough is because the enemy is holding on to our shirt, our pants leg, our coattail, pulling us in his direction. He doesn't want us going in the direction that was set in stone just for us by our Father!

So, don't give up or give in because the victory is yours, handed to you by our Lord and Savior Jesus Christ from the Cross! When you pray for strength, ask for it in the Name of Jesus, who said in John 14:14: *"If you ask anything in My name, I will do it."* ~NKJV

Ask for direction in His name; ask for wisdom in His name! By asking in Jesus' name, you pull yourself free from the grip of the enemy! You allow the enemy to see that he doesn't stand a chance against He that is in you!

When we submit to God's will for our lives, the same power that resides in Christ lives in us through the Holy Spirit. So, when the enemy puts the feeling of "giving up" in your flesh, think about how grateful we are that Jesus didn't give up on us when He fulfilled his destiny on the cross for our eternal benefit.

I pray God's blessing for you in strength, wisdom, and direction on your journey in Christ. In Jesus' name.

Amen.

WEEK SIX
Cast Off Your Feelings of Unworthiness

"When Simon Peter saw it, he fell down at Jesus' knees, saying, "Depart from me, for I am a sinful man, O Lord!" Luke 5:8 ~NKJV

"I'll go to church one day but I'm not ready yet. You know, I'm getting myself together. I got a few things I'm working on, and then I'm joining a church. Give me a chance to get my life together; then I will talk to the Lord."

These are common excuses of those who believe that they must somehow perfect themselves before joining a church or submitting to God's will for their lives. All too frequently we feel we that we have to "'fix'" ourselves before coming to the altar.

The word "'fix'" is defined as—to "repair" or "mend" what has been broken. It can be applied to a clock, car, or maybe even a refrigerator. But can we actually fix ourselves? Well, we all know we were created by God. And the way He created us, we cannot be fixed; not by man or ourselves. We were made to be transformed, not repaired. This transformation comes from being healed, and healing comes from God.

When it is put this way, can there be any reason to prolong our submission? There is no reason to wait to bring our burdens to the Lord because there is nothing we can do about them anyway except to submit to the Lord in obedience to His Word. God alone is the healer, and with this knowledge we can come to Him as we are.

In the opening scripture to this devotion, Peter has just witnessed a miracle. He and his fellow fishermen have been fishing all day and caught nothing. And against his better judgment, he followed the command of Jesus and threw his nets in the water one more time. Experience had taught him that relying on his own knowledge and skill, he would catch no fish, but against everything he knew, he followed Jesus' direction and he and his fellow fishermen caught an abundance of fish.

By casting their nets and catching an abundance of fish, Jesus allowed Peter and his companions to see what their purpose was. They would now follow that same command and bring men to the Lord, but now they would be casting their spiritual nets—God's Word!

As Peter and the other fishermen did, leave all your burdens at the altar. Deny yourself, as Jesus says in Matthew 16:24, and take up your cross and follow Him! Don't wait to try to "'fix'" yourself. Step out of your boat and let God's purpose for your life heal you. When you are healed, know that all that you are is God's will for your life in making you a disciple!

May God continue to bless and strengthen you on your journey in Christ Jesus. In Jesus' name.

Amen.

WEEK SEVEN
God Has a Plan for You

"I know the plans I have for you," announces the LORD. "I want you to enjoy success. I do not plan to harm you. I will give you hope for the years to come." Jeremiah 29:11~ NIRV

When I was in middle and high school, I played football. I was so good that I thought I had a chance as a starter in college, and even began thinking about a career in professional football. That plan ended when I attended a college that did not have a football program.

Other opportunities in my life came along that led me in many different career directions but they were not what I saw myself doing. In other words none of them felt like a calling. Yes, there were things I really liked doing and was very successful in my accomplishments, but I had to come to terms with whether or not they were God's will for my life, or my selfish desires.

"God's will" is what I consider a "calling." I think of a passionate desire placed in my heart by God. None of what I had done before or was doing in my life at the time resembled a calling. Sometimes I took what I liked or what I may have thought I was good at and believed it was my desired life's work.

You see, we may be a great doctor, lawyer, educator or may be exceptional in any other profession, but if God's plan is to direct those gifts toward an entirely different occupation, then we must allow it, for He did not create us without having a plan for our lives.

Jeremiah clearly says that God already has plans for us. It is a purpose and plan that He put together for us long ago. In fact, Ephesians 2:10 says, *"For we are His creation, created in Christ*

Jesus for good works, which God prepared ahead of time so that we should walk in them." ~HCSB

This promise of God is valid for those who walk in Christ. Our direction on this path of purpose comes from staying in God's Word. We may have many skills that lead us to think that we know our own destinies but make no mistake; God has already charted our course.

Now we must let Him prepare us for the task He created us for, and when we do, it will blow our minds. We must let go of what we selfishly think is our life's work and lean on God's will for our lives. To learn what He has for us, Jeremiah says in Verse 12, that we only need to ask direction: *"Then you will call out to me. You will come and pray to me. And I will listen to you. When you look for me with all your heart, you will find me."* ~NIRV

May God bless you with strength, healing, and wisdom on your journey in Christ. In Jesus' name.

Amen.

WEEK EIGHT
Accept God's Gift of Faith

"And He said to her, "Daughter, your faith has made you well. Go in peace. Your suffering is over." Mark 5:34 ~NLT

Before my transformation, it was hard for me to trust in God and in what He could do for me. I was conformed to this world, so when I read scripture, I didn't retain its message. And, lacking a message, I wasn't able to receive a revelation from God. My faith was weak.

It took God's Word, coupled with a terrible motorcycle accident, that caused considerable pain and suffering before my faith was strengthened. That day, I felt that the miracle of His healing hand healing me from my injuries, both those from the accident as well as the long-term pain caused by my addiction to alcohol.

One of my missions in life is to teach the Gospel so that others who cross my path don't have to suffer a tragic accident in order to strengthen their faith. We can be like the woman who was healed by Jesus in the opening to this devotion.

This woman had suffered from bleeding for 12 years. In Mark 5:26, the scriptures say that she had *"…suffered a great deal from many doctors, and over the years she had spent everything she had to pay them, but she had gotten no better. In fact, she had gotten worse."* ~NLT

We suffer and endure trials daily. Sometimes it seems that no matter what we do, things never get better, and for some of us, our situation gets worse. But God blessed this woman with a gift, the gift of faith. She had heard about Jesus and believed that all she had to do was touch His robe.

She didn't doubt, she didn't worry, and she didn't even feel the need to ask Him to lay hands on her. She simply had the faith that all she had to do was touch His garment. When she did, she was healed instantly. The Bible says in Mark 5:26: *"Immediately the bleeding stopped, and she could feel in her body that she had been healed of her terrible condition."* ~NLT

You, too, have that gift from God! He has given you the gift of faith! With this, you too, can begin to feel the blessing of God's power in your life. His healing; His power to restore what has been taken from you; His power to provide the warmth, covering, and security of His love that is renewed every day!

But first you must believe. You must have strong faith nourished by His Word. As you receive your blessing, thank the Father for His Son, who will say to you, "…your faith has made you well. Go in peace. Your suffering is over."

May God grant you peace, strength, and wisdom on your journey in Jesus' name.

Amen.

WEEK NINE
As We Are Comforted, Let Us to Be of Comfort

"All praise to God, the Father of our Lord Jesus Christ. God is our merciful Father and the source of all comfort. 4 He comforts us in all our troubles so that we can comfort others. When they are troubled, we will be able to give them the same comfort God has given us."
2 Corinthians 1:3-4 ~NLT

I used to be a long-distance runner, and I enjoyed a good run, especially in unfamiliar places where the scenery was new to me. There were many days when I didn't look forward to a long run. But it was the "runner's high"—the exhilaration I felt after the run—that motivated me.

While running the miles of hills, switching from asphalt to soil, speeding up and slowing down, in my heart and mind I could anticipate when the run would come to an end, at which point I would catch my breath, sit down, and give my legs a rest. Only then would I be able to enjoy the lift after the run.

Similarly, as Christians, we should look forward to a lift after our trials, and we know it will come because scripture tells us that God is our merciful Father and the source of all comfort.

The opening to this devotion begins by giving praise to God! It tells us that we should wake up in the morning praising God and go to bed praising Him. We praise Him because we are thankful for what He has done for us in our lives; we are thankful for the comfort he has brought us after the trials we've endured. Reminders of that comfort enable us to endure troubled times because we know that what God has done before, He will do again.

Often, we let the present troubles and trials overtake our memory of the miracles that have occurred in our lives. But we need to remember, not only for our motivation but for the motivation of those whom God puts in our path.

My addiction to alcohol put my wife and others through troubled times, and as a result, I now have the gift of knowledge of the pain they endured. God saved me and my marriage through an obedient, praying, wife who stood in the gap for me. I also have the knowledge of forgiveness, mercy, and healing.

This is the comfort that God provides us all. It is this goodness, this comfort, that must be shared with those who are experiencing struggles we have overcome. The experiences we have had and been brought through must be used to save another, as scripture tells us, "…we will be able to give them the same comfort God has given us."

May God grant you the strength, knowledge, and wisdom as you walk in your purpose in Jesus' name.

Amen.

WEEK TEN
Discipline Your Flesh in the Word

"Rejoice in our confident hope. Be patient in trouble, and keep on praying." Romans 12:12 ~NLT

Patience is one of the fruits of the spirit that I've had to work on. In one sense, I consider myself a patient person largely because my work requires patience to listen and find solutions to problems.

In my personal life, I often fail in being patient. For instance, getting stuck in traffic causes me to lose patience, which leads to anger. I also can lack patience in spending time with my children after a hard day at work. This impatience leads to selfish ambition because I want "me time" instead of spending time with family. Don't get me wrong, sometimes, we need that personal time to regroup. But "me time" should not become a ritual. God wants all the time we can give Him to seed into our children through us. This is why He blessed us with them. The enemy whispers impatience in our ears because it benefits him.

These outgrowths of impatience—anger and selfish ambition—are among the works of the flesh, according to Galatians 5:19-21. These shortcomings were leading to my downfall, to my spiritual death. How did I work through this? I "…rejoiced in hope…"

We must remember the times when God pulled us out of the dark places we found ourselves in. We have to remember how He healed our hearts after enduring brokenness and living in pain. To "remember" this is to "know" that He will do this again. And when we live in knowing that God will take care of us, we believe in what we don't see and what we believe in our hearts! We are living in the "hope"!

Like food for the nourishment of the body, the Word of God is needed daily for the nourishment of the spirit. During this transformation, we must stay strong in disciplining our flesh. As we stay in God's Word, the Holy Spirit will become stronger and help us keep that flesh disciplined.

And lastly, we must remain forever in prayer. We must pray for strength to endure the trials of our lives. We must pray for direction as we stay in God's Word and seek His guidance in living out our God-given purpose for the Kingdom.

God loves us so much! Let us love Him back by living the life He created us to live. By training ourselves in being obedient to His Word; rejoicing, being patient and praying every day!

May God continue to bless you with His strength, endurance, and wisdom to continue the mission of His Son Jesus Christ. In Jesus' name.

Amen.

WEEK ELEVEN
Curb the Power of the Tongue

"Let the words of my mouth and the meditation of my heart be acceptable in your sight, O Lord, my rock and my redeemer."
~Psalm 19:14 ESV

The Bible speaks about the power of the tongue, and it is up to us as Christians to watch what we say. As we read the Word daily, and as the Spirit grows stronger in us, we must be careful not to confuse the spirit by speaking into existence how we feel. Rather, we should speak into existence our spiritual intent.

I remember a time in my life when I said something that was received in such a negative way that afterward I had a feeling of regret, wishing I could take back what I had said.

But the words out of my mouth, however hurtful, degrading, improper, or foul, I cannot take back. At the very least I can ask for forgiveness, but as God's children, why would we even allow ourselves to speak with an undisciplined tongue? While the enemy is often blamed, we are more often the ones responsible.

Our flesh is strong. Strong enough to cause us to "speak our minds," say things like, "I'm gon' keep it real, let the chips fall where they may"! But as Christians, we must remember who we represent. We must remember who sacrificed for our salvation. We must remember that our God wants to do a great work in us, and we owe Him our very best in representing the Father and the Son! And that includes the words that come from our mouths.

One of the best ways to discipline our tongues is to wrap our words around the fruits of the Spirit as cited in Galatians 5:22-23. We must make sure that our words:

- Are spoken with love, peace, gentleness, and kindness
- Come from a place within us that is full of goodness
- Are formed patiently
- Are delivered to others gently and with self-control
- Are always spoken with the intent to spread joy

This is what we must strive for so that what we say, as well as what we do, is always acceptable in God's sight. God's light shines bright in those who seek the Father, and in seeking the Father, we must imitate His Son's love in everything we do. Let us begin with how we communicate with each other. We do this in the name of the Kingdom.

May God give you strength, courage, wisdom, and protection on your walk in Jesus' name.

Amen.

WEEK TWELVE
Seeing "The Horse in the Stone"

"For the message of the cross is foolishness to those who are perishing, but it is God's power to us who are being saved."
~1 Corinthians 1:18 HCSB

I remember a short story I was told when I was younger about a sculptor being complimented by his work on a statue. A passerby said to him, "This is amazing work! How were you able to make such a magnificent statue of a horse from this stone?" The sculptor replied, "The horse was there all along. I just chipped away the pieces that were not necessary."

Even as a youth, I understood that the sculptor saw the image he wanted to create through the coarse stone. Even if he had told the passerby before he started work, the man still would not have envisioned what the sculptor had.

In the same way, God gives us revelation. He gives us visions in dreams, in meditation, and in answered prayers that allow us to see His plans for us. Jesus did the same when he performed miracles but knew that non-believers would find the miracles incredible had they not witnessed them. For this reason, He would caution those whom He had healed not to tell anyone (Matthew 8:4; Mark 7:36). In other words, He wanted them to first understand that the power of healing came from the Father through Him so that others could witness the Father's power in them through their own actions.

By the same token, we as Christians must not allow others to take credit for what God Himself has done through them. God's miraculous power and blessings in the storms of our lives are not easy to explain to others who may witness them.

Sometimes, as we receive them, we find ourselves asking, "Really God? How could this happen?"

But we should have joy in knowing that what sets us apart from nonbelievers is that we are chosen! God has blessed us with the Holy Spirit that allows us to feed our faith, and He continues to teach us. We trust and believe that God will do what He said He will do.

So, don't get discouraged when you find yourself telling others about what God is doing in your life and they have a hard time believing it. Don't allow some to try to talk you out of believing. Hold on to His unchanging hand, and He will lead you down the path He created for you.

Just like those miracles that Jesus performed in the New Testament, God will perform the same miracles in your life. Soon, others will see the "horse in the stone."

May God give you strength, courage, and wisdom on your journey in Jesus' name.

Amen.

WEEK THIRTEEN
Accept Your Blessing and Be Healed

"But Elisha sent a messenger out to him with a message. "Go and wash yourself seven times in the Jordan River. Then your skin will be restored, and you will be healed of your leprosy." 2 Kings 5:10 ~NLT

In the Old Testament, Naaman was a warrior who had great admiration from the king he served. But for all his skill as a warrior, Naaman had leprosy. Following advice, he went to meet with the prophet Elisha from whom Naaman learned what he had to do to be healed of his condition.

The instructions were clear, and the actions required were simple. But as simple as they were, Naaman became angry and refused to follow them. Ironically, his anger stemmed from simple selfish reasons and ego. He complained that Elisha would not come out to see him in person, and that the waters in the Jordan River weren't suitable for him to bathe in!

We might ask "What's wrong with Naaman? A blessing is right in front of him!" But how different are we as Christians? How often is the answer, the solution to our healing right in front of us, and we choose to refuse it for selfish reasons and ego? I once remember weighing as much as 285 pounds. I had high blood pressure, sleep apnea, and was diagnosed as borderline diabetic. A nutritionist advised me what not to eat and how to exercise in order to prevent from becoming a full-blown Type 2 diabetic.

Just like in Naaman's situation, the answers were right in front of me. I had the knowledge, but what was I willing to do? Would I follow the advice? I couldn't give up the foods that were bad for me. If I had a choice between a salad and a pork chop with gravy, onions, and mushrooms, I would take the pork chop. I was shortening my life span, and I knew it, but my will to do what was best for my health was weak.

Naaman walked away angry until one of his officers stopped him with the words: *"…if the prophet had told you to do some "great thing," would you not have done it? How much more should you do it when he only tells you, "Wash and be clean"?* ~2 Kings 5:13 ~CSB

Finally, Naaman does what he had been told and is healed. He understood and became willing to do what needed to be done. You see, your blessing is right in the middle of what you are willing to do. Meditate and live in God's Word. Be mindful of His instruction and feed your spirit so that you are willing to do what God instructs you to do.

May God continue to bless you with His strength and wisdom on your journey. In Jesus' name.

Amen.

WEEK FOURTEEN
Sing God's Praises (Even When You Don't Feel Like It)

"I will praise You, O Lord, with my whole heart;
I will tell of all Your marvelous works.
I will be glad and rejoice in You;
I will sing praise to Your name, O Most High.
When my enemies turn back,
They shall fall and perish at Your presence."
Psalm 9:1-3 ~NKJV

There was a time in my life when I attended church and refused to stand, sing, wave my hands, or stomp my feet if I didn't feel like it. Where did that refusal come from? I don't know. Maybe it was because of situations in my life that kept me from recognizing God's goodness. But what I know about God now, makes me ashamed of how I withheld my praise simply because of stubbornness, pride, and foolishness.

I reflect on everything my Lord and Savior did and does for me, yet I couldn't give Him the praise He deserves. In 2 Kings 5:10, Naaman was told to do a simple thing by washing in the waters of the Jordan River seven times, but for his own selfish reason, his anger led him to refuse, nearly depriving him of his blessing.

Let us not miss our blessing by not giving God the praise we owe Him and His Son! As Christians, we can't thank Him enough, can't praise Him enough, and we can't show our gratitude enough, so why not sing and give praise to Him whenever we can, despite how we might feel!

The miracle of God's power in us is available to us when we rid ourselves of all doubt, fear, anger, and stress. And we give strength to that power when we shout and sing praises in Jesus name! Then we, and those around us, will feel God's presence, power, and healing that will guide us through our trials, suffering, and pain.

Even when we don't feel it, we should stand up and clap our hands! Even when the enemy is whispering in our ear, we must stomp our feet to make him flee! And when he tells us that we can't go on any longer, we must shout a joyful praise to the Father to let the devil know that he doesn't own us!

God is an awesome God, and with Him, all things are possible! Let God hear how you feel about Him by praising Him with all your heart! God loves you! Return that love to Him!

May God continue to keep you covered in His strength, wisdom, and healing power on your journey in Jesus' name.

Amen.

WEEK FIFTEEN
The Lesson of the Fiery Furnace

"If we are thrown into the blazing furnace, the God whom we serve is able to save us. He will rescue us from your power, Your Majesty. 18 But even if He doesn't, we want to make it clear to you, your majesty, that we will never serve your gods or worship the gold statue you have set up."
Daniel 3:17-18 ~NLT

Often when in prayer, we have in mind what we want. We ask God, and pray that He delivers on what we desire as well as on what we need. The Bible tells us to ask, so we do. But we must understand that we can't tell God how to bless us, especially when He knows what we need.

After all, what we ask for may satisfy us for a season, but what God has for us is not only for the good of the kingdom, but works for the eternal good of all who love Him, according to Romans 8:28. When we know this, then we can have faith that our prayer will be directed toward the good of all; and we don't have to know the end result of the blessing. This is why Shadrach, Meshach, and Abednego said, "…But even if He doesn't…"; they were speaking of being delivered from the fire.

So often we put limits on our faith because if we can't picture "how" God is going to save us, our minds won't accept being saved and the result is fear. Our three believers are simply saying they let go of trying to figure out how God was going to save them. Even if they could not conceive of the idea, they knew the God they served would rescue them no matter what.

They were pledging their faith in God, that in whatever He decides, they know it will be for the good of the kingdom, that He loves them enough to deliver them His way and in His time. We must embrace that faith as we go through our own trials.

Yes, we may enter the furnace with the coals at their hottest, but God will not let the enemy's weapon prevail. Make no mistake about it, as it says in Isaiah 54, the weapon may be formed against you, it may even be executed, but it will not succeed in its mission against you!

Look at the example of the three believers in the fiery furnace. The furnace, or weapon, was formed against them; fire so hot that it killed the men that were stoking it, and Shadrach, Meshach, and Abednego were sent in to burn alive. But standing on their faith, God did not allow any harm to come to them.

Therefore, wherever you may go, and whatever trial you are going through, you are not alone. Jesus is with you on your journey. The faith of these three servants shows us God's power through faith. Believe in Him and what He sacrificed for us to have eternal life.

May God continue to bless you on your journey in Jesus' name.

Amen.

WEEK SIXTEEN
Be Patient Through Your Trials

"When you hope, be joyful. When you suffer, be patient. When you pray, be faithful." Romans 12:12 ~NIRV

When you endure any trial or suffering and know that it was God who brought you through it, you acquire a new boldness about you. You begin to understand that the journey you are on cannot be traveled by you alone.

The expressions led by "I," we no longer have to voice anymore: "I don't know what to do!" "I'm stuck; where do I go from here?" We adopt new proclamations such as, "Thank you God for healing my marriage!" We pray in thanksgiving before the blessing itself arrives: "Thank you, Lord for the financial blessing you are about to bestow on this family!" Now, we know that God is our guide, our protector, and our healer. This life journey was orchestrated for us by Him, and by Him must be led.

Therefore, when we "…hope, be joyful." Allow the Holy Spirit to feed the joy given to you by God through what you have endured. The Spirit will then intercede on your behalf and pray for the blessing that God has custom made for you.

Throughout your trials, you must be patient, for there are lessons to be learned, things that need to be seen with new "eyes" of the Spirit that indwells you. God will use them to bless others along your path.

When you pray, do it with boldness, doubtlessness, and worry-free conviction! Strengthen your faith in God's love, power, and mercy for the purpose He created you for! Filled with this scripture, the opening verse continues: "…share with God's people who are in need."

Remember always that the power of Jesus' strength at the cross is in you. It is this power that will help you endure everything and anything that this world attempts to throw at you, keeping you away from the promises of God.

When God grants you victory over that, it is your duty to pass that power on to those whom God places along your path so that they will be able to continue on their mission, just as you have been empowered through Christ.

May God continue to keep you, guide you, and protect you on your journey in Jesus' name.

Amen.

WEEK SEVENTEEN
Show Others the God in You
(So That Their Eyes May Be Opened)

"…I am sending you to them 18 to open their eyes. I want you to turn them from darkness to light. I want you to turn them from Satan's power to God. I want their sins to be forgiven. They will be forgiven when they believe in me. They will have their place among God's people."
Acts 26:17-18 ~NIRV

My son watches everything I do. Not only my actions toward him, but how I raise his sister; how I love his mother, and how I comport myself around others. I pray that my actions plant the seeds for spiritual growth in him.

For my prayers to be answered, my life must be directed by the Word of God, not by my emotions and selfish desires. I say this because on the day that I decide to let my spiritual guard down and act out in my own way, the enemy will prop my son up for a front row seat, allowing him to see, through his daddy, that acting in ways that are not of God is "all right" and normal. To keep the enemy away from my family, I have to continue to live my life as God intends.

This way of life is also true for all who come into our orbit. God wants to use us as His vessel. So that when He places certain people around us, He can bless them through us. God wants us to, "…turn them from darkness to light…from Satan's power to God…" In Acts, He says, "…I am sending you to them…" Now, we often think of others as crossing our paths when God is actually allowing us to cross theirs. And when He does, it is an opportunity to show others God in us! What a great honor! The Lord is allowing me, despite everything I've done in my past, to represent Him! So, what do we do with that Good News?

It's easy to be a vessel under good circumstances. But what about showing up and representing the Father when you cross paths with someone who is angry and doesn't reply with a kind word?

That is when we must meditate on the scripture that says, "I am sending you to open their eyes." Your actions, your Christ-like personality will show them something that the enemy tries very hard every day to keep them from seeing. But because you are in their presence, God is there, too. His touch and His words are present to transform those whom He puts in your path.

God says in his Word that [He wants] "...their sins to be forgiven when they believe in Me." That belief will come in how we act, respond, and speak. So, live with godly intention.

When you do so, you are allowing God to use you, to transform those whom He puts in your path, so that "...they will have their place among God's people."

I pray God's strength, wisdom, and guidance on your journey in Jesus' name,

Amen.

WEEK EIGHTEEN
Obey the Father's Commandments
(to Keep You Free from Trouble)

"If someone claims, "I know God," but doesn't obey God's commandments, that person is a liar and is not living in the truth."
1 John 2:4 ~NLT

A father tells his son not to play in the street. The son understands him and assures him that he will not go in the street. When the parent is not looking, the son believes he has the freedom to do as he pleases because there is a chance that he will not get caught.

When I was younger, I took those kinds of chances. Sometimes I got away with it, and trouble ensued. As parents, it can be disappointing when we know that our children know what not to do but do it anyway. As parents, we have our reasons for setting ground rules.

Our Father in heaven also has ground rules and He has already laid our paths out for us. His commandments exist for the purpose of fulfilling His promise for salvation. They exist for Him to use His power in us for the good of the Kingdom. By not following them, we are in danger of falling short of God's promise of life, the promise born of the blood of His one and only Son. This danger begins to surround us when we live in disobedience, when we find ourselves living through the flesh, causing us to fall short of the paths that we are intended to take as described in Galatians 5:19-21 and include:

- Showing hatred
- Being promiscuous
- Engaging in idolatry

- Harboring jealousy
- Giving in to anger
- Pursuing selfish ambitions
- Exhibiting sexual immorality

1 John 2: continues, *"...But those who obey God's word truly show how completely they love him. 6 Those who say they live in God should live their lives as Jesus did."* ~NLT

Let us live according to the fruits of the Spirit in love, joy, peace, patience, kindness, goodness, faithfulness, gentleness, and self-control. (Galatians 5:22-23) When we wake every morning, let's meditate on one or more of these fruits and carry it in us throughout the day.

Let's not allow the world and its influence to take that fruit away from us, for these fruits will keep us out of the "street" and its associated dangers, and on the righteous path to salvation, a path that includes others whom God will bless through us on our journey.

May God keep you safe and covered in Jesus' name.

Amen.

WEEK NINETEEN
We Are Transformed by Our Suffering

"We now have this light shining in our hearts, but we ourselves are like fragile clay jars containing this great treasure. This makes it clear that our great power is from God, not from ourselves. 8 We are pressed on every side by troubles, but we are not crushed. We are perplexed, but not driven to despair. 9 We are hunted down, but never abandoned by God. We get knocked down, but we are not destroyed. 10 Through suffering, our bodies continue to share in the death of Jesus so that the life of Jesus may also be seen in our bodies."
2 Corinthians 4:7-10 ~NLT

After my motorcycle accident, I learned that it was necessary for my transformation. The "old" me had to die before the "new," "spiritual" me could be born, a process that involved a lot of healing.

The healing was not only physical, i.e., from the scars and broken bones of my physical self, but also from the emotional scars inflicted by tearing away of the worldly desires of my flesh. This healing process would discipline my flesh to be obedient to the Holy Spirit so that I could learn to walk the way of the Lord.

From this testimony it should be obvious that this transformation was not under my control, and I am glad that God's grace and mercy allowed it to occur in me. He brought me from a place I could not leave on my own.

We may cry at night, not knowing how we're going to make it through. We may have our own limitations, but know that there is no limit to God's power, for He knows the desires of our hearts. He created us for a purpose and has provided in us everything we need to endure, but first we have to trust, accept, and know that with Him all things are possible.

The text says that "the light …is from God…not from ourselves," meaning that our outer flesh is fragile and weak and is vulnerable to the destruction and desires of this world, but because of God's saving grace and mercy, He has provided us with a "light" that shines in our hearts!

It is this "light," this power, that enables us to, "…not be crushed when pressed; not be driven to despair when perplexed; never be abandoned by God when hunted down and not be destroyed when knocked down."

In our suffering, *"…we continue to share in the death of Jesus so that the life of Jesus may also be seen in our bodies."* It is from the fruits of the victory from our suffering, that others will see God's work in us. With this, we can declare His presence in theirs!

May God cover you and allow peace, strength, and direction on your journey in Jesus' name.

Amen.

WEEK TWENTY
You Are a Star

"And Abram believed the Lord, and the Lord counted him as righteous because of his faith." Genesis 15:6 ~NLT

This text is a part of God's covenant to Abraham, (The Abrahamic Covenant). In the beginning of this chapter, the Bible says that the Word of the Lord came to Abram in a vision. God told Abram not to be afraid. God said, "I am your shield; your reward will be great."

Abram responded to the Lord with a question, "Lord, what good are all your blessings when I don't even have a son?" Abram was very old and had no offspring to pass on all he had.

God told him in Verses 4 and 5, *"…you will have a son of your own who will be your heir. Then the Lord took Abram outside and said to him, "Look up into the sky and count the stars if you can. That's how many descendants you will have."* ~NLT

My friend, YOU are one of those stars!

The Bible says that immediately after God told Abram this, he believed what God promised him. His belief was confirmed by God when He "…counted him righteous because of his faith." Abram was counted righteous because he trusted in God and had no doubt or fear.

Again, I say you are one of those stars! You are a descendant of Abram! This means you are also an heir to God's promise to Abram! Believe, and receive that you are protected and that your reward will be great!

Today, whatever it is that you pray for in Jesus' name, claim it and believe in it so that you too will be counted as righteous!

You, too, will receive the promise God has for you! Believe and receive that your reward will be great because you are an heir to the binding covenant of God and because the Word of God says so in Genesis 15:1-6!!! Hallelujah!!!

Because of his faith and commitment to God, Abram was renamed "Abraham" by God. Allow this text to empty you of all that feeds any doubt and fear that you may have. Let this text release all in you that clouds God's direction in your life and receive this Word for today so that you can ready yourself to be counted as righteous because of your faith.

May God continue to bless and keep you covered and healed as you receive His gift of wisdom on this day. In Jesus' name, I pray.

Amen.

WEEK TWENTY-ONE
Remain the Soldier You Were Chosen to Be

"You therefore must endure hardship as a good soldier of Jesus Christ. 4 No one engaged in warfare entangles himself with the affairs of this life, that he may please Him who enlisted him as a soldier."
2 Timothy 2:3-4 ~NKJV

At times I give my son instructions for a task, such as taking out the trash, cleaning the kitchen, or maybe taking his bath earlier than usual. Occasionally, he will resist these tasks because he has something else in mind he would rather do. As the child in this situation, he only has limited knowledge about what I am seeking to instill in him.

As his father, my intent is to teach him. You see, God chose my wife Yolanda and I to be his parents, and there are intentions the Father wants to seed into our son through us. As parents, we were chosen to give to our son, and as our child, our son was chosen to receive from us. Whether he likes what we are attempting to teach or not, the seed is for his growth and benefit for the Kingdom.

Sometimes, we adults react in the same way during our Christian walk. We face our trials and sufferings with limited knowledge about the purpose for which we are going through them. But God has His own intentions for those times, and when we are able to endure these tribulations, we invariably find comfort, satisfaction, and relief as the reward from our trials.

In the Spirit, we have been chosen and given an assignment. This assignment has a purpose that will result in victory for the Kingdom if we complete it. But there are always worldly influences whose mission is to disrupt the completion of the assignment and they will fight tooth and nail to ensure that the victory is not won.

Therefore, we must stay focused on Jesus, the Son, whom we were given by the Father, (John 10:27-30) and endure what the world attempts to throw at us. Like a caring parent teaching his child, God already knows where we are going and it is a good place. A place that He has prepared for us through His Son. We must believe from the strength of our spirits and not be deterred when we were once, according to Timothy, *"... entangled with the affairs of this life..."*

God has enlisted you for a task, a mission, and a purpose. A task custom-made just for you with the promise that you will have victory in it. So, trust in Him and receive the victory that is already done in the name of Jesus!

May God continue to bless you, keep you, and give you direction on your mission for the Kingdom in Jesus' name.

Amen.

WEEK TWENTY-TWO
Be a Conduit for God's Blessings

"When it is in your power, don't withhold good from the one it belongs to. 28 Don't say to your neighbor, "Go away! Come back tomorrow"— when it is there with you."
Proverbs 3:27-28 ~HCSB

I am blessed to have four beautiful children. Eleven years separate my two oldest from my two youngest. Without question, I am the father of all of them, equally. But the difference in ages among them has shown me the difference in the kind of father I was to my two oldest when they were growing up compared to the father I am today with my two younger children.

One of my failures as a father to my older children was that I did not devote the time to them that I should have. When they were growing up, I was enlisted in the Army and was away from them a lot, but when I was home, I still didn't give them the time and attention that I should have.

For instance, after coming home from military exercises, I would look forward to time by myself. My daughters would ask me to play games, go to the park, swimming, or anything else that involved my undivided attention, but all I could think about was my time to watch TV, and time for drinking in short, my "me time." What I didn't realize was that God had blessed me with children so that He could seed into them through me. To make this happen, I lived under the same roof with them for 18 years. But as we all know, 18 years can come and go quickly!

According to Proverbs 3, we aren't to hold back what God has given us to seed into others. It is His blessing to give, not ours, to be passed on to those whom he puts in our path. The example above describes my relationship with my oldest girls. I was selfish, thinking about my own desires and it kept me from imparting the fatherly teachings God wanted me to instill in them.

This failure can also be applied to our relationships with co-workers, church members, and friends—anyone whom we take for granted. It includes that individual whom we think talks too much and try to avoid. Yet, he is a child of God, too, and if we find ourselves continually in his presence, it could be that God is trying to bestow a blessing on that person through us.

I now live every day trying to be the best father I can be for my two youngest children. Because of that effort, my relationships with my two eldest ones and my grandchildren are much stronger.

As Proverbs admonishes us, we are not to *"withhold good from the one it belongs to…"* Allow God to use you at every opportunity that He can. After all, it's an honor to be chosen by the Father. Live your life as a conduit for His blessings.

May God keep, protect, guide, and provide wisdom for you on your journey in Jesus' name.

Amen.

WEEK TWENTY-THREE
Let Go of Your Mind-set of Sin

"For the mind-set of the flesh is hostile to God because it does not submit itself to God's law, for it is unable to do so." Romans 8:7 ~HCSB

Growing up during my middle school years, we lived next to an interstate overpass. For safety, it was restricted from the neighborhood residents by a metal wire fence.

My friends and I would climb the fence and play in a ditch that lay at the bottom of the hill next to it. Enjoyment for us was playing in the water where some frogs lived. The danger of where we were playing never entered our imagination.

One day, my father yelled for us to get out of there. He took me inside and told me never to climb that fence again. And just like any middle-school-aged boy, I said OK. But the next time I got the chance, I was back over the fence and in the creek with the frogs and my friends.

This anecdote shows just how strong the mind-set of sin is. The world teaches the young to ignore doing what is right simply because doing wrong is so much easier. This mind-set leads one to believe that what we are doing is OK as long as it hurts no one.

My father had the responsibility to protect me from what I didn't see, from what I couldn't imagine: vehicles moving at 80 to 90 miles per hour just a few feet away from me, as well as the dangers of bacteria and organisms living in the water invisible to the naked eye. Most importantly, he had the responsibility for training me to mind and to do as I was told.

This lesson applies to us every day in our Christian walk. Our Father in heaven gives us orders and direction in His Word to follow and lots of times we fall short. How our mind-set fights that! We are told that others will look at us differently, will consider us weak, and will not respect us for complying with this act of righteousness commanded by the Father.

When we give in to that mind-set, we give others power over us and over the gift God created in us. We can't allow that to happen. We must let God help us change our mind-set so that we do the right thing, no matter what the world tells us, or what the consequences may be. This mind-set will tame our flesh to do as God tells us. We must continue to walk as Christ would walk so that the seeds of love, light, and life will germinate in those whom God places on our path.

Let God heal you and let Him use you. Shift your focus from those who surround you and keep it on God. The Father, the Son, and the Holy Spirit will show you the way.

May God keep you covered, healed, protected, and filled with the wisdom of the day on your journey in Jesus' name.

Amen.

WEEK TWENTY-FOUR
Let God Act on Your Behalf

"The Lord shall fight for you, and ye shall hold your peace."
Exodus 14:14 ~KJV

We often give into our flesh and act on emotions triggered by other people or situations. We allow these opportunities to feed into what we say, what we do, and lead to actions that we may regret later.

The scripture *"…and ye shall hold your peace…"* means submission to God and includes trusting Him to act on your behalf against the negativity that impacts you. In your obedience you are covered; in your stillness you are protected, and through your suffering, God will reveal Himself in you through your strength.

Therefore, you must not react to others when ridiculed, chastised, or abused. This is hard to do because the world has taught you that you will look weak if you don't, you will look stupid if you don't, and you will not be respected if you don't. Putting God first may make this a little easier to do. For instance, you might say, "God would not like me to 'say' what I'm thinking in this situation. He would not want me to 'do' what I'm thinking about doing in this situation."

This is the appropriate response for a Christian because God has other plans for His children who stay still in His peace during such stressful situations. He accompanies and heals them; while at the same time, He fights that battle for all who believe. Now, the enemy doesn't want you to know that; he wants you to continue in your anger.

God wants you to live in peace, knowing that He will hold you close to Him! *"No weapon formed against you will succeed…"*

(Isaiah 54:17) because your submission affords you His protection. He will take on that adversary for you so that you don't have to. Watch the Lord turn your pain, stress, and suffering into a blessing that not only will save your life but also the lives of those he places in your path! When you think you look weak, others will witness God's power and presence in you.

This is a miracle only God can bring, and He brings it with His grace and mercy, which is renewed every morning! (Lamentations 3:23) If we are going to live like Christ, if we are going to be who God created us to be, we must do as Jesus did and be still during those times of pain, suffering, and confrontation. Bless those that curse you, and allow God to fight for you. While it may be hard, remember that you were created to endure and you represent the Most High.

May God keep, bless, and comfort you as you continue to walk in Jesus' name.

Amen.

WEEK TWENTY-FIVE
Let Us Love Through Action and in Truth

"Little Children, let us not love in word or speech, but in action and in truth." 1 John 3:18 ~CSB

The days of despair come often and it doesn't matter whether they arrive before a blessing or after one. Despair will always be that "uninvited guest." All too often I am faced with bills that become overdue. I am that man, that head of household, who, like many are faced with a situation where there's "too much month at the end of the money."

I am the one to whom my wife looks to make things right, and the feeling of falling short is embarrassing and hurts. But I am also that man who has made sacrifices to walk the path that God has laid out for me. A path that my wife and I have agreed on and one from which we will not depart. So what do I do when that uninvited guest comes around and tries to bring me down? I look to the Word of God, of course.

You see, I not only teach the Gospel, but I have learned to live it. And living it brings the perks of provision. For scripture says in 1 John 3:18 that we must love, *"…in action and truth."* Tony Evans echoes this in his commentary: "What your lips proclaim, your life must support."

When we act in this way, God will provide covering. The times when we fall into despair, stress, or doubt are when our hearts take us away from God's promise to provide for us. We who feed our spirits with the Word begin to think that we are abandoning our belief in God for feeling unworthy of His grace and mercy during these times.

But when we love through action and in truth, we are covered and assured of God's grace and mercy. When we love others and dedicate our time and talent to those in need, God not only voices His approval through those He heals through our efforts, but He also provides for us when we doubt whether we will make it through the month.

Accordingly, when you love in action and truth and not just talk about it, God works miracles through you. Because He is glorified through you, you will be glorified by Him! When you believe that, you no longer have doubt, worry, or fear.

You are able to rebuke the enemy every time he sends an unwanted guest to try to destroy what Jesus has built: your marriage and your relationship with your children. To love one another through action and truth is the Lord's command.

Remain in Jesus. Let this be known by your actions, and others will see Jesus in you.

May God continue to bless and keep you on your journey in Jesus' name.

Amen.

WEEK TWENTY-SIX
You Are Protected

"And the Peace of God, which surpasses every thought, will guard your hearts and minds in Christ Jesus." Philippians 4:7 ~HCSB

Is there a memory that haunts you, that keeps you from fulfilling your full potential? You may ask, "What do you mean?"

You may walk the Christian walk, love your spouse, and try and raise your children in a godly manner but something you've done or said in your past keeps you from being your best self for the Lord.

Be encouraged! God wants us to know that when we submit to His will for our lives, we don't have to allow the past to imprison us, preventing us from seeking righteousness. According to Pastor Kenneth Copeland, "…Jesus has unlocked the prison doors of guilt that have kept you captive…" Don't be that free mind that stands in a prison behind an unlocked door.

You can embrace your new freedom because scripture says in 2 Corinthians 5:17 *"Therefore, if anyone is in Christ, he is a new creation; old things have passed away, and look, new things have come."* ~ HCSB

God has forgiven us! He has shown it through the sacrifice of His One and Only Son, so we must trust in God's love for us and His will for our lives in order to let the past go.

As you learn and embrace God's love, you will know His peace. Memories of your past will be transformed from terror to testimony, a testimony that will save someone's life.

"How do I learn this peace?" You might ask. According to Philippians 4:8 *"…whatever is true, whatever is honorable, whatever is just, whatever is pure, whatever is lovely, whatever is commendable—if there is any moral excellence and if there is any praise—dwell on these things."* HCSB

As you dwell on these gifts from God, your new freedom will allow you to become the tool that He has customized for your purpose in life. All you need to do is, *"…do what you have learned and received and heard and seen in me, and the God of peace will be with you."* Philippians 4:9 ~HCSB

May God continue to keep you strong in His peace on your journey in Jesus' name.

Amen.

WEEK TWENTY-SEVEN
Cast Aside Unworthiness: Be Strong in Faith

"...Just say the word from where you are, and my servant will be healed." Luke 7:7 ~ NLT

How strong is your faith today, at this very moment? In the midst of what is going on in your life, how strong is your faith? You may be facing financial issues, your children may be causing you trouble, or maybe your spouse is acting in a way that affects the sanctity of your marriage.

In other words, you may be facing things that you believe are impossible to overcome. But I am here to tell you that God loves you and wants you to have your heart's desire in Jesus' name. Therefore, we must live our lives knowing that God loves us and that He wants to bless us with abundant living!

That means with financial stability, Godly marriages, and strong families. He has prepared it all for you and desires that you have it. The first step in receiving these blessings is believing in them, in having the faith that God's Word is final and true.

In Luke 7:7, a centurion sends some respected Jewish elders to ask Jesus to heal his slave. Jesus went with the men, but just before they arrived at the house, the soldier ordered some men out to stop them with the message that he, the officer, was not worthy of Jesus coming into his home. He said that he was not even worthy of the honor of meeting Jesus and merely asked if Jesus would, *"...say the word from where you are..."*

I love Jesus and need Jesus in my life every day; yet here is a man who could have met Jesus face to face but deemed himself unworthy. And in his humility, he asked Jesus to *"...say the word..."* The soldier had faith that his prayer would be answered. That was his faith on that day. Again, I ask you, how is your faith today?

Jesus responded in Verse 9, turning to the crowd to say, "…I tell you, I haven't seen faith like this in all of Israel!" When the officer's men returned to the house his slave was completely healed.

I live my life feeding my faith with the Word of God every day because, as a child of the Most High, I want Jesus to be pleased with my belief in His sacrifice.

I pray and ask in thanksgiving because I want God to know that He has a prayer warrior, a testimonial preaching and faith-walking servant in Billy Jackson! That light in me spreads to my family and from them to the community they encounter. So, from now on when you are asked the question, "How strong is your faith?" Reply, "Centurion strong!"

May God's peace surpass your thoughts and guard your hearts and minds in Jesus' name.

Amen.

WEEK TWENTY-EIGHT
Come to Know God
(Who Has Given Us Everything We Need)

"By His divine power, God has given us everything we need for living a godly life. We have received all of this by coming to know Him, the one who called us to Himself by means of His marvelous glory and excellence."
2 Peter 1:3 ~NLT

I can remember once during my middle school years going into the kitchen and telling my mother I was hungry. Dinner wasn't ready, so she told me to fix myself a sandwich to tide me over. I'd just come in from school and football practice, so I ate a sandwich, but it didn't fill my need.

Later, when dinner was ready and I sat down to eat, I realized that I wasn't that hungry. The sandwich actually did satisfy my hunger need. You see, the way our bodies are set up, it takes only a few minutes for the stomach to alert the brain that the body's need for nourishment has been filled.

God created us like that. Lots of times we have needs in life and we pray to God to fulfill them, just as I had a need to satisfy my hunger. A seed is planted in the name of your prayer, but periods of time must elapse for that seed to germinate. Often, we would rather satisfy our need quickly rather than wait for the blessing, an action that results in spoiling our blessing.

But when we lean on patience, we fall in line for the blessing because, as scripture says, *"…God has given us everything we need…"* This is where our faith and trust and come into play because we just have to allow the process to unfold. Had I known that the sandwich would spoil my dinner, I wouldn't have eaten it.

Giving in to our fleshly desires can spoil our blessings in the same way. But we can avoid it by receiving this wisdom from "coming to know God." When we do so, we find everything we need in His Word. As Verse four continues, *"...He has given us great and precious promises. These are the promises that enable you to share His divine nature and escape the world's corruption caused by human desires."* ~NLT

When we know better, we can walk better in Christ's name. We must always remember that when we are "going through," "...God has given us everything we need for living a godly life..."

Read and meditate on God's promises; then embrace what He created in you so that you won't be pulled in by the enemy's influences. You will then be equipped to avoid them. Remember, God loved us first and His mercy and grace is renewed every morning. Lamentations 3:23.

May He continue to guide, cover, heal, and grant you wisdom on your journey in Jesus' name.

Amen.

WEEK TWENTY-NINE
Always Pray with Enthusiasm

"For I desire loyalty and not sacrifice, the knowledge of God rather than burnt offerings." Hosea 6:6 ~HCSB

Have you ever been in a conversation with someone, and during the conversation you notice that what they are saying is rehearsed? For example, they speak to impress you, attempt to get a laugh, or speak in generalities. Maybe the person's focus is off, and the conversation becomes hard to understand. Either way, you find yourself in a one-way conversation that is not genuine or personal.

Do we do this in our conversations with the Lord? If so, they become routine, like brushing our teeth. We often do this without even being aware of it, and it affects the power of our prayer. We must be careful not to allow our worship of the Father to fall into a habit in which we are not fully present.

For instance, if you are standing in the gap for your marriage during a time of weakness, it's easy for the enemy to come in and test your resolve because your focus may be so distorted that your prayers may be rote and said without feeling. Before you know it, you're saying "Amen," and you haven't let the words of your prayer for your marriage penetrate to your heart.

In frustration you may wonder why your prayers aren't answered and why your marriage is in the same state as it was before you started praying. It's because your lack of enthusiasm has drained your belief in the very miracle that you have been praying for.

During these times, just hold onto God's Word expressed in Colossians 3:23: *"Whatever you do, do it enthusiastically, as something done for the Lord and not for men…."* ~HCSB

Just as in genuine conversation, you must engage enthusiastically and be fully present, so must you be fully present to the Lord every time you pray. You must also believe in the miracle for which you are praying.

Just as you would want someone's undivided attention when engaged in conversation, so does God want yours. He wants you to speak, pray, and believe with all your heart when it comes to calling on Him. Once this happens, miraculous fruit will result, and your blessings will be in full bloom!

Know with enthusiasm who you are praying to. Know with enthusiasm that God is God all by Himself. Give God your undivided attention, and watch His power flow into you!

May God continue to bless, keep, and heal you on your journey in Jesus' name.

Amen.

WEEK THIRTY
Allow God to Do His Best with Your Worst

"Instead, we have renounced shameful secret things, not walking in deceit or distorting God's message, but commending ourselves to every person's conscience in God's sight by an open display of the truth."
~2 Corinthians 4:2 HCSB

In the 1990s when my two oldest children were toddlers, I had a few bad habits that were noticeable to all whom I came in contact with—especially them. One of them was my addiction to alcohol. My addiction caused me to miss many school events that they were involved in.

It's not that I didn't care, it's just that I didn't understand the gravity of my addiction and its impact on those close to me. I wasn't conscious of the fact that I was seeding the wrong ideals and morals as a father to my children on a daily basis. There was no light in my walk in those days.

Today, I am a new creation in Christ, and my walk is different. My two youngest children get the benefit of my being the best dad I could ever be because of it. I thank God that I am able to make up for falling short with my two oldest children and that they have forgiven me, giving me a second chance.

As Christians, our walk is the same, no matter who is watching. We never know who God is going to place on our path, so we must be conscious of the "light," God's power and representation, in us.

Our "truth" is our walk in the fruits of the spirit, (Galatians 5:22-23). In everything we do, we must be guided by love, joy, peace, patience, kindness, goodness, faith, gentleness, and self-control. We must allow these to be our guides in maintaining our "light" while displaying Christ in all we do.

We must live to rebuke any day that attempts to make us fall short of the power of these fruits. It doesn't matter if we have had a bad day, or if we are tied up in traffic, or the way we feel after a long week. The end result is that God just may want to work through us on our worst day, during our weakest moment. So hold on to His unchanging hand, and allow Him to do His best with your worst!

We were all created for a purpose. We must let others see the God in us by living everyday knowing that He is with us in everything we do and that His love was first and is eternal.

May God continue to guide, heal, and protect you on your journey in Jesus' name.

Amen.

WEEK THIRTY-ONE
The Lifeguard with Us

"If the Lord doesn't build a house, the work of its builders is useless. If the Lord doesn't watch over a city, it's useless for those on guard duty to stand watch over it." ~ Psalm 127:1 NIRV

I remember my test day at the swimming pool being one of the scariest times in my life. I was four or five years old. It was frightening because I had to swim from side to side in the nine-foot depth of the pool.

I was terrified that there was so much water that I couldn't touch the bottom of the pool, but I remember my father kneeling down beside me and saying that the "lifeguard" was with me. He then added that, even if He weren't there with me as I swam, He'd be in the pool and wouldn't let anything happen to me. He told me to stay focused, and I'd make it to the other side.

Now, I realize that I wasn't by myself in that pool. My father was with me—my natural father and my spiritual Father. This anecdote reminds me that I've dove into many "pools" in my life and have fallen short because I entered them alone. Knowledge of the Word of God has made me aware that all those shortcomings had to do with my not following the paths that He had intended for me to follow.

As God has created us, He has also created our purpose and our path to that purpose, and He ordains a victory that is already set and done. We, as obedient children, must choose to pray for His guidance in the situations that God has allowed to happen in our lives.

For instance, I can say that my career objective is to be an entertainer or actor, but if God has not ordained it for me, all of the acting classes that I take won't make it happen and won't deliver the blessings that God has in store for me.

We can choose a profession and be extremely good and successful at it, but the victory and reward will be limited by our own desires and what our minds conceive our happiness to be.

But when we let go of our wants and needs and focus on God's intent for our lives, we are able to reap blessings that are beyond our imaginations. This is because God not only knows what we need but also what will bring us eternal joy.

When we pray for God's will in our lives, all our roles in life are blessed with His eternal abundance and love. Every step we take will be on the same path that He has created for us, and in that we can have confidence.

Be courageous, for our Lifeguard is on duty! May God continue to bless, keep, guide, and cover you on your journey in Jesus' name.

Amen.

WEEK THIRTY-TWO
Supplement Your Faith with Goodness

"For this very reason, make every effort to supplement your faith with goodness, goodness with knowledge, knowledge with self-control, self-control with endurance, endurance with godliness, godliness with brotherly affection, and brotherly affection with love."
2 Peter 1:5-8 ~HCSB

There was a time in my life when my health wasn't the greatest. I had high blood pressure, I wore a C-PAP machine to sleep, weighed 300 pounds, and was borderline diabetic. In October 2012, I made the decision that I was going to get healthier. It wasn't easy, but I did my research and learned how to train my body in what to eat.

Consequently, I lost 105 pounds, today my blood pressure is normal, and I have no indication of becoming a diabetic. One of the ways that I have learned to keep my weight in check is how I "break my fast" in the morning. Our body goes into starvation mode after four hours without food. It is during this period that it really matters what foods the body takes in first.

Let's say that a good night's sleep is between six and eight hours. Upon waking, you will want to eat or drink something that will be nourishing for you as well as easy for your system to digest. Freshly made fruit and vegetable juices fit the bill perfectly. I drink one every morning, and it has helped my metabolism handle my daily diet.

Just as we must have a healthy regimen for maintaining our physical body, we must address what we should do to become healthy spiritually. 2 Peter Chapter One gives us the blueprint for growing our faith and finding peace in the Word of God.

Verse 3 of Peter says, *"His divine power has given us everything required for life and godliness through the knowledge of Him…"* Continue to follow the text as it tells you how to grow in faith, a that faith must be "supplemented with goodness." The more you do good, the more you feed your faith, the more you allow God to use His power through you. But that goodness must be supplemented by knowledge. You must know the Word of God in order to receive direction as exemplified by Verse 5.

Everything you need is given to you in the Word of God. You need only receive it willingly and submissively, forsaking any fleshly desires for anything other than God's will for your life. Allow the faith that God gave you to grow and allow that peace to give strength to God's peace in your heart.

Let the peace of God, which surpasses every thought, guard your hearts and minds in Christ Jesus.

Amen.

WEEK THIRTY-THREE
Pray for Wisdom Through God's Word

"After Jesus said this, He looked toward heaven and prayed. He said, "Father, the time has come. Bring glory to your Son. Then your Son will bring glory to you." John 17:1 ~NIRV

An example of team success is when its members execute their specific tasks, mission, or actions, in one direction for an agreed-upon outcome. In football, if every member of the offense executed his one action for the play, the offense would be successful in scoring a touchdown or at least in picking up the yardage needed to be successful for the next play.

In our Christian walks, we must apply the same principle. Like football, we also have a coach who gives us our direction to execute our plays: Our Father. We must call on Him to direct us on our paths, and, like Jesus, we must pray continually.

We must pray for God's revelation in His Word, so that by doing so, we can become aware of His answer to our prayers and relate His Word to our trials, sorrows, and pain. In the Word, we find the strength and courage to push through as God pulls us through with His unchanging hand.

Let us understand that God has created us for the purpose of carrying His message. We do this equipped with the wisdom of his Word, applied to the trials of our lives. Wisdom does not come to us automatically. We must pray for it in God's Word so that we may be prepared to share it with those whom God places in our paths.

We must also pray for His healing power. Many of us carry within ourselves pain and memories of a life we've lived as unsaved beings. The enemy uses these memories and emotional pain to keep us in bondage, a bondage that allows the enemy to influence us. This influence may cause us to feel as though we are not worthy to be Christians.

We pray for God's healing power since we have been given the chance to receive eternal life through His Son Jesus Christ, who was hanged, bled, died for our sins, and rose on that third day for our salvation! This healing allows us to proclaim Him as the "Way," the "Truth," and the "Life"! When we claim this aloud, the devil will flee! (James 4:7)

While we never know what others are going through, God does. As His vessels, we must sustain our prayers to the Most High for the knowledge and wisdom He allows us so that when we receive a revelation from Him, we are able to act on it. Through each of us, He delivers a message of hope and peace to those He uses us to seed into.

May God continue to bless and keep you covered in His Son Jesus Christ.

Amen.

WEEK THIRTY-FOUR
Pray for the Protection of Others

"I am not praying that You take them out of the world but that You protect them from the evil one. 16 They are not of the world, as I am not of the world. 17 Sanctify them by the truth; Your word is truth."
John 17:15 ~HCSB

When I was led by my flesh, addicted to alcohol, I wasn't able to see God's truth. Not only did I not see it, but I also didn't want to see it. Often, when speaking at events or preaching, I confessed that I didn't even pray for myself and for deliverance from my problem.

But God loved me. And in His love, He placed people around me to pray for me. When others pray for you, there is nothing you can do about your transformation. I was in a place where I was too weak to control my situation, and God knew that, so He dispatched His angels for me.

Let me just say this: We might not like the way in which our transformation takes place, but if we submit during those times of struggle and pain, God will heal us in our weakness, giving us a strength that we never thought possible.

God performed a miracle in blessing me with a beautiful wife and family that prayed for me. It took a tragic accident for me to turn my life around, but a change did come! Yolanda ignored the world when it told her, "He ain't gon' change; he's an alcoholic; they never change…" What she had was faith in the Most High! She prayed in thanksgiving and celebrated the blessing, not focusing on what she could *not* see, but believing in what she could not see—God's promise!

Nor did she worry during the time it took for me to change, which happened a year and a half after her submission. During that time God assigned her a mission while He worked on me. Yolanda believed in the Word of God when He said that He doesn't want anyone to fall short of repentance.

Just as Jesus prayed for His disciples, we should also pray for those around us whom God has placed on our paths to train. During this training, He delivers His answers, direction, protection, and miracles through us who are obedient to Him in our walk in His Son's name.

Jesus said that He was not asking that his disciples be taken away from the world, but that they be protected from the evil influences of the world. The light that God powers in us guides others away from making poor decisions, having bad intentions, and embarking on fruitless journeys.

As Jesus prayed for others, let us also pray for others for whom we have committed ourselves to pray.

May God keep you protected on your journey in Jesus' name.

Amen.

WEEK THIRTY-FIVE
Remember What God Has Done for You

"I pray not only for these, but also for those who believe in Me through their message." John 17:20 ~HCSB

During my recovery period after my motorcycle accident, I had to be put to sleep whenever the doctors had to look at and treat my leg during its healing. Once I had healed enough for them to treat it without anesthesia, I was able to see my leg for the first time since the accident.

When they took the bandages off, I was horrified at what I saw. My leg looked like it had been mauled by a bear! It was bleeding everywhere and appeared as if all my skin had been torn off. I looked up, and the doctors were shaking hands and hugging each other as if they had completed a successful operation.

In a loud voice, I asked, "What's going on? Don't you see my leg? Is this the best you can do? This is terrible!" One of the doctors came to my bedside and explained that they could replace the tissue I lost in my leg with other tissue from my body and that they could take skin grafts from other parts of my body to cover what they had done, but that the healing had to come from somewhere else. The doctors explained to me that because of the blood circulating, my leg was on its way to healing! Now that was something to shout about!

I realized at that moment, that this was the message that Jesus had been praying for. You see, a non-believer could attempt to tell me all day long that the doctors had healed me, that the reason I am able to walk on my own leg is that the doctors did their job.

But as a Christian, I can correct them by telling them that the doctors could only operate; they could replace tissue, stitch, and bandage me up. Healing, however, would come from on High!

Because the transplanted tissue had taken and had not been rejected, my leg began to bleed and the blood circulated like it was supposed to! "By His Stripes I am healed!!!" This is what Jesus prayed for when He said, *"...for those who believe in Me through their message..."*

Your weakest point is where God's power lies. When you are at the point where you can't do, God can! This, brothers and sisters, is where your message is born! Born in the belief of the Savior!

Remember what God has done for you because that is the real message. When the time comes, He will place someone in your path who will be blessed by the testimony of how He brought you through, how He performed a miracle in your life, and that message will save somebody's life.

May God keep you protected in His wisdom and direction as you walk in Jesus' name.

Amen.

WEEK THIRTY-SIX
Condition Yourself Through Spring Training

"The Lord isn't really being slow about His promise, as some people think. No, He is being patient for your sake. He does not want anyone to be destroyed, but wants everyone to repent."
2 Peter 3:9 ~NLT

The one thing I did not like about football was spring training, the time when we would come to practice, way before the season started, to begin our conditioning. Day after day we would work out, doing push-ups, jumping jacks, running relays, sprints, and long-distance with no game in sight. In other words, no quick rewards for all the work we were putting in.

But when the season rolled around and it was time to put those uniforms on and hit the field, we were unstoppable. All that conditioning and training during the off season paid off because we were ready. We were strong enough to withstand any team we played.

When you are going through your trials and you find yourself saying, "Why Lord?" Think of it as your "spring training" for your blessing. You see, the Lord has a huge blessing for you, but He won't give it to you until He knows you can handle it. This "wait" time is our preparation time.

The opposing team of the enemy prepares non-stop to shatter everything God intends for us in His will for our lives. God's promise to us is real and done! We may think that God is slow to deliver on His promise to us, but in actuality, He is allowing us to get conditioned through our trials so that when we endure the pain, suffering, and sorrow; when we stand up, we are ready to face any spiritual adversary. We are conditioned spiritually.

So, when we find ourselves saying, "I'll go to church when I get myself together," or "I don't think I'm ready yet to seek the Lord; I need to fix myself," understand that the Lord is waiting to accept you just as you are. You can't "fix" yourself. God made you, and only He can "fix" you. That impossible situation is an opportunity for God to reveal Himself to you and everyone around you.

God wants everyone He created to have a chance at the eternal life provided by the sacrifice of His One and Only Son. He did not create us to be destroyed. His desire, in His love for us, is for us to repent. The time frame for our submission to our walk in total obedience to Him is His time, not ours.

And when that perfect work is done in us by Him, we will receive the reward of His promise. So hang in there and endure because His promise for you is already done.

May the Lord continue to bless and keep you on your journey in Jesus' name.

Amen.

WEEK THIRTY-SEVEN
Rely on Godly Weapons to Defeat the Enemy

"Look, I have created the craftsman who blows on the charcoal fire and produces a weapon suitable for its task..." Isaiah 54:16 ~CSB

I don't like using the word "fear," so let's substitute it with the word "issue." I used to have an issue with heights. Being up high and looking down brought out feelings and emotions in me that would sometimes cause me to freeze in my tracks. But even though I had this issue, I was always able to complete any task that was in front of me.

One example is related to my military service. I was a crew chief on a UH-60 Blackhawk helicopter. It involved me not only performing maintenance, but also flying aboard the aircraft during missions.

I had to secure myself with a harness and hang out of the aircraft while it was in flight. I attended Air Assault School, where I learned to rappel out of a helicopter more than ninety feet in the air, jumping out feet- and sometimes headfirst. All of this for someone who had an issue with heights!

Believe it or not, I did it. To this day, I feel a little queasy going up in high places, but I now have control of my issue with heights. How have I conquered it? God has given me the tools I need within myself to see my tasks through, no matter what my situation may be.

In Isaiah 54, God is telling Israel that He loves them and *"... will not become angry or rebuke…"* them again (Isaiah 54:9). He is teaching them in this text that He has angels creating the weapons we need for His will to be done. For that very purpose, some of those tools were instilled in us who believe.

It doesn't matter what your issue may be in any given situation. God has given you the means to overcome it. The enemy will gladly use fear to deter you from your journey in Jesus' name, but you must remember that the issue comes from the enemy's influence in the first place, and we have the strength, through the power of God in the Holy Spirit, to overcome it.

As I have with my issue regarding heights, you must stand in defiance of yours. Show the enemy that what God has given you is stronger than what he has given you from the world! (1 John 4:4) Use the weapon that God has armed you with. You will find that it is *"...suitable for its task..."*

May God continue to bless and keep you on your journey in Jesus' name.

Amen.

WEEK THIRTY-EIGHT
Resist Temptation: Arm Yourself with the Word

"Then Jesus left the Jordan, full of the Holy Spirit, and was led by the Spirit in the wilderness for forty days to be tempted by the devil…"
Luke 4:1-2 ~Tony Evans CSB version

The scripture says, *"…led by the Spirit…to be tempted by the devil…."* First, we must recognize how the world is trying to influence our minds. Scripture already says in James 1:13, *"…God is not tempted by evil, and He Himself doesn't tempt anyone."*

Evangelist Tony Evans teaches that being under the influence of the Spirit does not mean uninterrupted peace and tranquility. But why is Jesus in the wilderness? Jesus was the "second man" or "last Adam." In 1st Corinthians 15:45 it says, *"The first man Adam became a living being, the last Adam became a life-giving spirit."*

Evans presents a different perspective. The devil tempted the first Adam and succeeded in having him kicked out of the garden into the wilderness. The "first Adam" was on defense and lost, but the "last Adam" played offense and won. Empowered by the Holy Spirit, He went into the wilderness to face the devil so that He might return humanity to the garden.

In the wilderness, Satan held out three temptations; in response, Jesus quoted three passages of Scripture. When the devil couldn't take it anymore, he departed. This teaches us that sometimes in our lives we need to challenge the enemy with scripture. As Jesus did with the devil, we must crack open the Bible in the face of the enemy.

When we are tempted to anger, discouragement, jealousy, and adultery, we should rely on scripture and challenge the devil in our moment of physical weakness with the question, "What does God say about what you are telling me?" When you do, it throws God's Word in the devil's face, knocks him off his game, and reminds you that the enemy can't defeat the spiritual weapons that God has armed you with. If you keep using the Word of God as your ammunition, sooner or later the devil will yield to it.

As believers, you will also experience a spiritual relief. The enemy will surround you with worry and stress while you face that temptation. But when you resist it with God's Word thrown in the enemy's face, God's peace will settle upon you like water on the parched earth and the worry will disappear.

Jesus prepared for the battle with Satan as he fasted. When he went to war, he was prepared. He relegated the physical to the background, pushing the spiritual to the foreground. Prepare yourself as well. Make sure that you are armed spiritually if you are going to engage in spiritual warfare and emerge victorious.

May God continue to arm you with strength, courage, and wisdom on your journey, in Jesus' name.

Amen.

WEEK THIRTY-NINE
Change Your Attitude and Follow God's Will

"One day long ago, God's Word came to Jonah, Amittai's son: "Up on your feet and on your way to the big city of Nineveh! Preach to them. They're in a bad way and I can't ignore it any longer." But Jonah got up and went the other direction to Tarshish, running away from God." Jonah 1:1-3 ~MSG

This is the famous story about Jonah and the big fish. Let's take a closer look at this story, as it has a very powerful message. At first glance, we think this story is about Jonah and his trial with the fish, but when we really look at it, it is all about God and His love for His people.

God had a plan for the Ninevites. But all Jonah could think about was how evil and sinful the place was. Do we do that? When God calls on us to do something, do we have our ways of running from God? Do we respond: forgive me Lord, but I can't stop using foul language, making angry outbursts, drinking alcohol, smoking, or going to places that are not of God?

We hear God telling us to change directions and go the other way but we, like Jonah, run in the opposite direction from God. Jonah thought he could run far from God's will by going on a ship, but he ended up being swallowed by a fish.

God's will for us is deep— so deep that we may not comprehend His "end-game" in our lives, but we have to see it through. Jonah's attitude had to be adjusted by his being locked in the belly of the fish for three days. It was only then that he was ready to accept his calling.

My big fish was a serious motorcycle accident. Being in the belly of that situation changed my whole attitude about God's will for my life. Yes, I still go through a journey of the unknown but God has proven to me time after time that if He brings me to it, He will bring me through it. This is because God's love for us is the ultimate love we can know. What is your big fish? What are you trying to run away from? Heed the call of your Father on High before you are swallowed by your "big fish."

In the text, God wants Jonah to deliver the message to the sinful city that in forty days "…Nineveh will be destroyed…" Why do you think God gave the city forty days, when He could have destroyed it right then? It's because He wants us to have the chance to repent, (2 Peter 3:9). Because the people of the city saw the error of their ways and quickly repented, God spared them destruction.

How wonderful it is to know that God loves us so much that He gives us a chance to repent from whatever sin we have committed! Take this chance to repent before you encounter your "big fish."

May God keep you in His grace on your journey in Jesus' name.

Amen.

WEEK FORTY
The Importance of Instruction

"Hold on to instruction; don't let go. Guard it for it is your life."
~Proverbs 4:13 CSB

The other day, I decided to mount a bracket for a television in our son's room. Now, in case you are unfamiliar with mounting a bracket or attaching anything heavy to a wall, you have to find the stud, the wood framing, behind the wall in order to ensure that the mount will hold. Well, I took it upon myself to drill into the wall until I found it. Needless to say, I drilled about four holes in the wall and never found the stud to attach the bracket to in order to mount the TV securely.

For fear that I might drill too many holes in the wall, I got smart and bought a stud finder, a battery-operated device to help me find the stud. The stud finder "senses" the nails securing the drywall to the stud. Once I found the studs, I was able to attach the bracket and mount the TV.

What I want you to see in this anecdote is that I had no idea what I was doing. All I saw was me mounting a TV, but forgot I was doing it for the first time. In other words, I was approaching a task without any direction. Once I researched the task and obtained the proper equipment, I was able to find success in my mission.

Think about that the next time you feel uneasy about the actions you perform on your journey in Jesus' name. When we meditate on the Word of God, we receive instructions for our task. From that direction we are able to perform our task successfully.

The times when we feel we are at our lowest are the times when God is giving us the strength and wisdom, we need to perform the task we are called to do. Heed these times, because they are the times of greatest instruction.

No matter how the world responds, following instruction from the Word leads to success. When our lifestyle is Christlike, and we are in the Word daily, God will direct our paths. We just have to show up in the position, instructions in hand, and allow God to use us.

You might be a minister who did not get the reaction from the congregation you had hoped for. Family or friends may treat you differently because you now live your life in Christ, but have no fear or doubt. We must know that the instructions and direction from the Word is for God's power of seeding others through us. We may not see the fruit from those seeds, but beautiful fruit will grow.

That's right, God is using us for His plan. The path has already been prepared, but in order for us to follow it, we must receive instruction and direction from His Word. It is all a part of His plan for our lives that He made long before we were born.

May He keep you and continue to guide and protect you in all that you do in Jesus' name.

Amen.

WEEK FORTY-ONE
Discipline Your Flesh to Live by the Spirit

"For the wages of sin is death, but the gift of God is eternal life in Christ Jesus our Lord." Romans 6:23 ~CSB

Because of my accident, I needed to change my diet. The injuries to my leg would decrease the amount of cardio exercise I was used to doing to keep my weight down. To pursue a healthy lifestyle, I had to eat differently. Over time I trained myself to eat within a certain time frame, and I cut out the consumption of foods that were not good for me. It worked well until the holiday season of 2020.

I began to invite my old eating habits, and before I knew it, I was eating everything that I had cut out of my diet before. I tried to check myself by vowing that I would fast for the next couple of days but could not resist my cravings. Like an alcoholic who takes a drink after a long time of sobriety, I bit into food I had tried to stay away from. The cravings that I thought I had mastered began to master me again.

On my birthday, January 7th, I decided to discipline my flesh once again. I talked to my wife about my plans so that I could have accountability with her, and I prayed to God for strength and determination. To this day, I have reclaimed the strength in my spirit and my flesh is no longer in control.

The sin that the scripture talks about is a form of quitting. Even with the mind-set of knowing better and doing better, it is still easier to follow the path of least resistance—the path of the desires of the flesh—than it is to follow the Holy Spirit. Why? Because we have had practice giving in to the flesh since birth.

We do so because we have not practiced finding peace in situations where our flesh makes demands on us—a peace that is God's love and will for us. It is hard to feel the love of God when we let someone or something else take His place and when we become fixated on what the flesh is calling us to do. And that makes it easier to put our desires before God's will.

Yes, the discipline of the flesh may be difficult at first, but when we strengthen our spirits with the Word of God and live by the Holy Spirit in God's will, it becomes easier for us, and we can control our tendency to give into the flesh.

Let us discipline ourselves in the Holy Spirit. Just because the journey may seem hard, it doesn't mean that it can't be accomplished.

May God bless and keep you in His will on your journey in Jesus' name.

Amen.

WEEK FORTY-TWO
Purify Yourself: Be Who God Created You to Be

"Now in a large house there are not only gold and silver vessels, but also those of wood and clay; some for honorable use and some for dishonorable. 21 So if anyone purifies himself from anything dishonorable, he will be a special instrument, set apart, useful to the Master, prepared for every good work." 2 Timothy 2:20-21 ~ CSB

When I was growing up, my grandmother had our "everyday" dishes for our daily meals. But when we had company, she would pull out the "good dishes" to make a good impression on our "honorable guests." This was her way of presenting to guests our very best. God does the same thing with His children. When we are ready, He presents us to others as His best.

Looking at the text and seeing "wood" and "clay" juxtaposed with "gold" and "silver" one might say, "That's me…I'm just ordinary, nothing special. That's my place in this world." But that is not true. God made us all for a purpose. And in that purpose, we all have a distinct value. That value sets us apart from what the world may consider valuable.

First, consider the words "wood and clay." In Isaiah 53:2, according to Jesus' appearance to those who viewed him, *"…He didn't have an impressive form or reflect majesty compelling us to look at Him, no appearance that we should desire Him."* Sometimes we feel as though we are not worthy or don't "shine" like others around us. But just like Jesus, God has given us a purpose. And with that purpose His power will be shown in you in His time.

Second, the meaning of "wood and clay" could also be found in the act performed by the children of God. In John 13:5, Jesus performed an act that during that time was below that of a king—washing the feet of others.

As a sergeant in the U.S. Army, I had to and assign tasks that needed to be done. One of those assignments was cleaning the latrine. I noticed that some of my soldiers were making fun of the other soldiers who were performing the task. Instead of disciplining them, I got down on my knees and pitched in to help the soldiers assigned to the job. The action brought new meaning to them. There I was, superior in rank to them, performing the lowliest of tasks.

When Jesus knelt at the feet of His disciples, he is showing us in an ordinary "wood and clay" act that all of us can serve, no matter what our station in life. As Dr. Charles Stanley puts it, "The message here is that every task God gives us is important to His kingdom," no matter how lowly it is perceived to be. When the task is done in the name of Jesus, it is worth more than "gold and silver."

May God continue to allow His peace to surpass your thoughts and guard your heart and mind in Jesus' name.

Amen.

WEEK FORTY-THREE
Endure Through Your Suffering

"When a woman is in labor; she has pain because her time has come. But when she has given birth to a child, she no longer remembers the suffering because of the joy that a person has been born into the world."
John 16:21 ~CSB

We all know that one traffic light we run into on the way to work, home, or to any road on which we travel by car daily. As we approach it, and it turns yellow, we drive a little faster because we know if we don't make it through before it turns red, we'll be sitting there for a long time.

Too late! The light turns red, and we are stuck. Every word that's not in the Bible comes to mind because we don't like being stuck at the light. Then, something amazing happens: the light turns green. Most of us don't realize it but after the light turns green, we pull off and continue our drive, never to think about that light again—until the next time we have to come that way.

All the stress we went through while waiting for the light has gone. We made it through the delay and the worry is gone. It's the same with life when we're going through our trials.

When we are suffering and enduring, the duration seems longer than it is. But that endurance builds character, and that character gives us the strength we need to receive our blessings from God. The example of the traffic light brings to light another thought.

Just as we forget the impatience we had while waiting for the light to change, in the same way we become impatient and we forget what God has done for us through our suffering during past trials and tribulations. There was a time in our past when we prayed, hoping relief would come. And what seemed like forever became a second when the Lord pulled us through.

The stress of the trial was transformed to newfound joy after the storm. It is important that we remember those times when we are stuck at our "red light" during our times of struggle. It will remind us that when we experience our next trial, that trouble doesn't last always. In this, we become stronger Christians.

John says that the pain exists because it is our time, but as soon as the spiritual fruits of that labor are born, we no longer remember the pain because of the joy birthed from our endurance. This joy will outshine all our misery and give light to a new direction leading us out of the valley we were in! We must always remember what God has done for us. Give Him a shout of praise for His grace, mercy, power, and forgiveness because He didn't have to do it, but He did.

May God bless and keep you in His will on your journey in Jesus' name.

Amen.

WEEK FORTY-FOUR
Accept God's Cover in Good Times and Bad

"As Pharaoh approached, the Israelites looked up and there were the Egyptians coming after them! The Israelites were terrified and cried out to the to the Lord for help." Exodus 14:10 ~CSB

Have you ever read stories in the Old Testament and wondered why the Israelites' faith was lost even after they had witnessed great miracles? For example, in Exodus, the Israelites had witnessed the power of God through the ten plagues and their release from slavery under the Pharaoh. Through Moses, God promised them their freedom, and through him they were bound for the Promised Land.

We read this, and say, "How could they doubt? With everything they just witnessed, how could they doubt God's love and power in setting them free?" In their defense, the sea appeared to be intimidating, but the situation of their being caught between the sea and the pursuing Egyptians can be a similar comparison to the seemingly impossible trials and obstacles we face in the world today, showing how, with God, all things are possible. COVID-19, like the Egyptians, has arrived as a worldwide pandemic that has come in full pursuit of humankind every day. We fear that it's going to infect us. Resignedly, many say that it's just a matter of time and that we all are going to contract it.

COVID-19 is our "Red Sea." But I'm here to tell you to shake that feeling of doubt and despair, for My Father says in 2 Timothy 1:7 that He, *"…has not given us a spirit of fear, but one of power, love, and sound judgment."* ~CSB

We must believe in Him and not lean on our own understanding. We must know and believe that God has already covered us in the blood of His Son Jesus, but that covering is good only if we accept it. How do we do that? By relying on what God has given us—the power to change what the enemy has convinced us is tragedy. The power to understand that God is giving us the opportunity to show Him how much we love and trust Him. The sound judgment we need to change our perspective about what's going on in the world today.

Yes, it is easy to give Him praise when our rent is paid, and when we are living our best lives. But we need to give Him the same praise during perilous times like these because when we accept the coverage, we are covered during bad times as well as in the good times.

Just as the Israelites couldn't have known that God would open the Red Sea for them to walk through safely, we have no idea how He's going to get us through today's calamity. Just believe, and give Him the praise and glory because nothing is impossible for our Father!

May God continue to bless you on your journey in Jesus' name.

Amen.

WEEK FORTY-FIVE
Renew Your Inner Self Every Day

"Therefore we do not give up. Even though our outer person is being destroyed, our inner person is being renewed day by day. 17 For our momentary light affliction is producing for us an absolutely incomparable eternal weight of glory." 2 Corinthians 4:16-17 ~CSB

In September 2013, I had an addiction to alcohol that I could not overcome, and it was destroying my health and my marriage. I had only enough discipline to abstain from drinking on Sundays because it required that I attend church and Sunday dinner, both of which obligations placed me in the company of my pastor, who also happened to be my father-in-law.

Consumed by the overpowering fleshly desire to drink, I knew that I was drinking myself into a slow but inevitable death. This caused my very soul to ache to the point that I couldn't even pray for myself. But when the Holy Spirit interceded on my behalf for my emotional healing, I became a victim of a near fatal motorcycle accident.

As a result, my right leg below the knee was destroyed. Although my ankle and foot were still intact, my knee was hanging by a tendon and everything in between…gone. Initially, the doctors informed me of their intention to amputate the leg. Regardless of that news, I knew I was alive! I had survived, I was in my right mind, and I had accepted their decision. I was full of joy because God had given me another chance at life!

My outer person was destroyed, but because the spirit within me had been joined to the prayers of my wife and others who were praying for me, the external was giving way to an internal reconstruction, resulting in a new me.

Now, as I look back on the eight surgeries that I had to undergo and all the pain I had to endure, it doesn't feel as though I had gone through a "momentary light affliction," but compared to the man I am today, it turned out to be just that!

The doctors were able to save my leg, and I am now five years free from the 105 pounds I had lost during my freedom from addiction to healthy living! I am now free from the high blood pressure that I'd had since the 1990s. To have experienced the miracle of having a craving for alcohol taken from me by the hand of God is an *"...absolutely incomparable eternal weight of glory..."!* No longer do I have the taste for it.

Our God is the God of the impossible. Whatever you may think you are facing today, God is much bigger than it! Trust in Him and not in what you see and hear. *"For what is seen is temporary, but what is unseen is eternal."* ~CSB

May God continue to cover you with His strength, wisdom, and direction on your journey in Jesus' name.

Amen.

WEEK FORTY-SIX
Your Testimony Is Your Strength

"…One thing I do know: I was blind, and now I can see!"
John 9:25 ~CSB

Throughout our lives God blesses us repeatedly. We tend to let the bad days, or the dark times overshadow our memories, and we forget the times of blessings. The enemy wants us to do that. He knows that when we remember the good days, the blessed days, the days God showed us that He is always there for us, we will become powerful in the Kingdom.

When we remember what God has done for us, it assures us that He will do the same again for us no matter what we are going through. It reminds us that He is the same God now as He was then, and nothing has changed about His power or His love for us.

Not only will that testimony strengthen us inside and neutralize all the negativity that this world tries to throw at us, it will allow us to testify to non-believers that the same God that exists in us, lives also in them. The power of that testimony comes when we speak with passion about what God has done for us regardless of the circumstances that surround us.

Look at the healed man in the book of John. The Pharisees, the leaders of that time, set out to discredit Christ. They were in disbelief that the man had been healed. They asked his parents, and they testified that their son had been born blind and did not witness Jesus healing him. In fact, they said in Verse 21, *"He is of age; ask him yourself…"*

They told the non-believers to go to the "source" of the story. "Allow him to convince you." When God places a non-believer in your path, He intends to use you to plant the seed of hope in that soul. God wants everyone to be saved and to come to the knowledge of truth (1Timothy 2:4). And this, my friend, is how God intends to use you daily in His purpose for you in the Kingdom. Don't be afraid. Stand ready for Him to use you!

The Pharisees told the man to give God the glory, not Jesus because they claimed Jesus to be a sinner. But the man replied, *"Whether or not He's a sinner, I don't know. But what I do know: I was blind, and now I can see!"*

Testify to how God brought you out of the blindness in your life and because of the blood you can now see! Give God the glory and praise because the Son came so that you might have life and have it more abundantly! Tell somebody your story and plant the seed of hope that God will water and fertilize.

The struggle that you are going through right now is a brand-new story, and when you share it, it will bear the fruit of blessings and bring hope, love, and strength to the lost soul that you will encounter on your journey.

To God be the glory, in Jesus' name.

Amen.

WEEK FORTY-SEVEN
The Treasures You Hold in Your Heart

"Don't store up for yourselves treasures on earth, where moth and rust destroy and where thieves break in and steal. 20 But store up for yourselves treasures in heaven, where neither moth nor rust destroys, and where thieves don't break in and steal. 21 For where your treasure is, there your heart will be also." Matthew 6:19-21 ~CSB

As I have dedicated my life to God's will for me, I've found that when I think of the things of heaven, I find that I no longer worry. I trust in God for the promises He's declared in His Word for my life. It's only when I focus on the things of this world that I begin to worry and doubt.

I find that I invest my emotions in things that can disappoint, things that can fail, things that can leave me and let me down. The world gives us nothing that can be considered solid when it comes to a promise.

For example, a man may have in his mind what he desires in a wife. This desire is born from what the man has learned from the world. As a result, the desire will bear fruit tainted by worldly standards and expectations. The man did not allow God to lead him in his desire.

Maybe it is the tendency of the world to disappoint us that causes us to feed the doubt and fear that we receive from it. After all, we didn't get those feelings from God. No. God gave us the Holy Spirit, and from the Holy Spirit we receive its fruits (Galatians 5:22-23). CSB

When we invest our emotions in the treasures of this world, we are setting ourselves up for failure. We are doomed to succumb to doubt, worry, and fear because we haphazardly put our faith in material things that can be *"…destroyed by moth and rust…"*

We idolize things we've bought, which can be, *"...taken by thieves..."* And when this happens, we are disappointed and left in pain. It is in this way that we are deflected from our mission in this world as Christ followers and the children of God.

But today we can make a change! Our hearts can be focused on a different treasure. *"...the treasures in heaven!"* The treasure of God's promises in our lives according to His will for us. And because of His Son who, before He hung, bled, and died for us, said in John 10:10, *"...I have come so that they may have life and have it in abundance."* ~CSB

Where is your heart? To what treasure is that love, deep inside you, actually directed? "For where your treasure is, there your heart will be also."

God bless you on your journey in Jesus' name.

Amen.

WEEK FORTY-EIGHT
Be Transformed by the Spirit

"We all, with unveiled faces, are looking as in a mirror at the glory of the Lord and are being transformed into the same image from glory to glory; this is from the Lord who is the Spirit." 2 Corinthians 3:18 ~CSB

The world has taught us that the sufferings we undergo must be blamed on someone or even at times, some things. The flesh gives us the selfish desire to claim innocence. Sometimes I've caught myself asking, "I'm a good man, why is this happening to me?"

When we become Christians, we put our faith and trust in God, but the inner workings of the flesh are still at work trying to defeat our spirit, causing us to blame God for our troubles. How often in life do we do this?

If we just allow the Spirit to teach us, to show us how to change our perspective, we will see that the trials we are experiencing are actually opportunities to prepare us for the blessing in store for us. Instead of seeing suffering as the flesh wants us to see it, we begin to see our transformation.

This transformation is needed because, when we were born, we were born in sin. But because of Jesus we were given an opportunity to prepare to become Christians. For some of us that might be enough, but for others, like myself, we needed more because even though we may have claimed Christianity years ago, we still lacked the faith of a strong believer.

In time and immersed in the Word, I began to pray for that faith. Because of it, my spirit interceded for me when I suffered trauma from my motorcycle accident. I could have allowed the flesh to overtake me and lived miserably, making others around me miserable because of my pain and physical impairment.

Instead, I held on to God's unchanging hand, knowing that He created me for a purpose. I realized that what happened to me was intended to transform me from who I used to be, to the man I am supposed to be!

As believers, we must recognize that what we are going through sometimes in our lives is not where we will always be in life. We must understand that we are only put in places at certain times in our lives to allow God to work on us and to work through us on those whom He has placed around us.

The next time the flesh wants you to blame someone or something for what you are going through, listen to the Spirit when it tells you, "It is not necessarily about what you are going through as much as it is *how* you go through it."

May God continue to bless you with His wisdom as you walk your journey in Jesus' name.

Amen.

WEEK FORTY-NINE
Wait for the Lord, and Put Your Trust in Him

"I wait for the Lord; I wait and put my hope in His word."
Psalm 130:5 ~CSB

The situations that we are living through now are truly trying. I told my children the other day, "I've been your age, but I did not live through a pandemic, so I can't give you advice according to my experience at your age."

We have endured staying at home and not being able to follow our normal routines. It is getting to the point now that some of us are reaching our limit and crying out, "I don't know how much longer I can do this!"

Our finances are being tried, our relationships are being strained to the breaking point, and our patience as parents is being tested to limits that we didn't even know existed! How much more can we take?

Well, I am here to tell you that God's being in control is real, and we should never lose faith in that. My spirit tells me that this is a time when God wants "His time" with every single believer. In other words, He wants us all to seek Him for direction during this season.

I believe that God is working in us, preparing us, and strengthening us. We must submit to His power in us by believing this truth while we wait. The Psalm says that we wait for the Lord and we do this because we are waiting on deliverance from all that is in us that is not of God.

This waiting period enables us to rid ourselves of idolatry, moral impurity, hatred, strife, jealousy, anger, and selfishness

(Galatians 5:19-21) as it strengthens us in our good fruits: love, joy, peace, patience, kindness, goodness, faithfulness, gentleness, and self-control.

This is important because the second part of the scripture says that we, *"...wait and put our hope in His word."* What is God's Word on this waiting period? In such scriptures as 2 Peter 3:9, where it speaks about the wait not being a "delay" as we understand delay in His promises. But it is because of God's grace, mercy, and patience that God does not *"...want any to perish but all to come to repentance."*

The time that we are going through right now is a period where God is delaying His judgment on us because He wants us to "get it right"! He wants us to have that chance to be with Him in the Kingdom! Understand and believe that this waiting period is not us waiting for God, rather it is Him waiting for us!

So, let's take this time, regardless of the effects of the pandemic to transform our hearts and minds to live in peace and love, knowing that God loves us and will not leave us.

May God continue to bless you in strength and wisdom on your journey in Jesus' name.

Amen.

WEEK FIFTY
Risk Being a Disciple, No Matter the Cost

"But Jesus told him, "Follow me, and let the dead bury their own dead." Matthew 8:22 ~CSB

If Jesus stood in front of us right now and said, "Follow Me," what would we do? Many would respond to the person asking that question, "Are you crazy? I would follow my Savior!" But, in reality, we may consider our jobs and our homes. What would really have us stressed out is leaving behind any and everything we've worked our whole lives for. Would we be willing to leave our legacies behind to follow the King?

In Matthew, Jesus was standing in the middle of a large crowd when a scribe came to him and told him he would follow Him wherever He went. Another told Him he would follow, but *"… first let me go bury my father."* (Verse 21)

In other words, the person wanted to receive their inheritance before committing to following Jesus. This is when Jesus, without hesitation, told him, *"Follow me, and let the dead bury their own dead."*

Pastor Tony Evans says in his commentary that Jesus was saying, "Let those who are spiritually dead worry about such things. Are you willing to risk discipleship even when it doesn't fit with your economic plans?"

When we are faced with the opportunity to serve as a disciple and are confused about leaving our comfort zones, we should ask ourselves: "What is it that this world has for me that is more important than what God has for me?" Think about this the next time you come to that spiritual fork in the road.

"But sometimes it's hard to know where God is leading me," you might say. But I tell you, if your decision comes down to something that is based on worldly desires versus something based on godly desires, look to Him, and the right choice will be in plain view.

You will be able to look to Him and ask. The Bible says in James 1:5-6 *"Now if any of you lacks wisdom, he should ask God—who gives to all generously and ungrudgingly—and it will be given to him. But let him ask in faith without doubting."* When you do this, you will see the right choice in plain view.

There is nothing of this world that can be of more value to us on our journey in Christ than what the Kingdom has prepared for us. And we will only be able to see it when we feed our spirits daily. So we must stay in the Word because God gives us direction through it. Be assured that it will become a lot easier to tame your flesh of its desires when you do.

May God continue to keep you and bless you on your journey in His Son Jesus' name.

Amen.

WEEK FIFTY-ONE
God's Promises to the Faithful

"Let us hold on to the confession of our hope without wavering, since He who promised is faithful." Hebrews 10:23 ~CSB

I attended Fisk University in Nashville, Tennessee, from 1986 to 1990, and I made some new brothers and sisters during my time there. These relationships have stood strong to this very day. I grew very much during that time, but I did not achieve my one goal: graduation. In December 1989, I became a father. The responsibility of being a single parent at that time made it difficult to continue my education, so I dropped out and sought employment to care for my daughter.

After leaving Fisk, I joined the military, started a family, and began a career in law enforcement. My resume grew with all of my achievements during that time, but although I had accomplished much in my life, I still had not earned a degree. Deep down inside, it was what I really wanted.

There came a time in my life when I desired to learn how to study the Word of God more, so I attended Emmanuel Bible College in Nashville. I was so immersed in my studies there, that before I knew it, I had earned a bachelor's degree in biblical studies from the seminary in 2017.

In my heart I held on to the "confession" that I had made to become closer to God and His Son, substituting my "wants" for what God wanted for me. I now wanted my life to be directed toward the path that God had prepared for me. It was when I leaned toward God's way and away from my way that the rewards bestowed on me by the Most High outweighed the suffering I had endured to get there (Romans 8:18). You see, not only did God allow me to earn my bachelor's degree in the year 2020, but He made a way for me to receive an honorary doctorate degree, become a professor, and teach at that very same school! What an awesome God!

We may think that where we are right now is where we will remain for the rest of our lives, but we do not have the whole picture. God's promises are true, and they override what the world is trying to embed in our consciousness every day.

We know that God will do what He says He will do, and when we focus on Him, the reward of His blessing will be upon us before we know it.

So, don't worry about a victorious outcome. God has already prepared that for you. He is faithful, and He will provide for you. Seek Him; be true to Him, and His will for your life will reveal itself to you.

May God bless and keep you as you journey in His Son's name.

Amen.

WEEK FIFTY-TWO
Claim the Strength to Move Mountains

"But when the kindness of God our Savior and His love for mankind appeared, He saved us…through the washing of regeneration and renewal by the Holy Spirit." Titus 3:4-5 ~CSB

It is written in the Bible how God's people have let him down many times. For example, we read in Numbers Chapter 11 where the Israelites were hungry and wandering in the wilderness when God provided "manna" from the heavens daily for them to eat. Yet the people complained, for they wanted fish and, *"…cucumbers, melons, leeks, onions, and garlic"*—foods they missed to the point of thinking about returning to slavery in Egypt for them. How crazy is that? To want to return to a terrible life from which God delivered them.

Even today, I can think about times when I was ungrateful because I wanted more than what I had. When I was blessed with my first car, I wanted a car that I thought was better. When I prayed for the money to pay my rent, God would bless me with rent and more, but I would spend it on something else.

Looking back, God has always kept a roof over my head and food on my table. He never held me accountable for my shortcomings when it came to my having faith in Him. Instead, He blessed me, and it all began when He decided to save us all. God's plan to allow us a chance at eternity, to undo what Adam did in the garden, came with the sacrifice of His One and Only Son, who would be born and *"…become flesh…"* (John 1:14).

His birth would be the beginning of life for us all! As told in the Old Testament of Isaiah 9:6: *"For a child will be born for us, a Son will be given to us, and the government will be on His shoulders. He will be named Wonderful Counselor, Mighty God, Eternal Father, Prince of Peace."* ~CSB

This is a gift from God because He not only loves us so much, but He loved us first. He loved us enough to give us a chance to get it "right" through His Son Jesus. All we have to do is accept His Son as our Lord and Savior and believe every day, no matter what the world may throw at us, that through the Son, God is able to give us the strength to move mountains.

When these mountains are moved, we can claim our inheritance, which will be our place in the Kingdom that Jesus has prepared for us who believe. He did this, *"...through the washing of regeneration and renewal by the Holy Spirit."* I pray the blessings of Christ to you this Christmas.

May the Father cover you in His grace, mercy, and wisdom as you continue on your journey in Jesus' name.

Amen.

SCRIPTURES FOR FURTHER READING

Week 1: Isaiah 55:8-9; Lamentations 3:26

Week 2: Psalm 107:9; Psalm 145:19; John 4:14; John 6:27

Week 3: Mark 4:19; 1 Timothy 6:17; 1 John 2:15-17

Week 4: John 6:51; 1 Corinthians 10:21; Hebrew 10:29

Week 5: Isaiah 42:1; John 17:4-5; John 17:24-26

Week 6: 2 Samuel 6:9; Revelation 1:17; Revelation 22:8-9

Week 7: Psalm 33:11; Micah 4:12; Hosea 3:5

Week 8: Mark 5:29; Acts 14:9; Luke 17:19, Matthew 9:2

Week 9: Philippians 1:6; 2 Corinthians 2:14; Exodus 18:19

Week 10: Hebrews 10:36; Romans 15:13; Psalm 62:8; 1 Peter 4:13; James 5:7; Hebrews 6:12

Week 11: Psalm 119:108; Psalm 66:18-20; 1 Peter 2:5; Hebrews 13:15

Week 12: 1 Corinthians 2:14; 2 Corinthians 4:3; Hebrews 4:12; Acts 13:41; 1 Thessalonians 1:5

Week 13: Exodus Chapter 14; Daniel 3:8-30

Week 14: 1 Chronicles 16:24; 1 Chronicles 16:12; Revelation 15:3; Psalm 51:15; Isaiah 12:1

Week 15: Acts 5:29-32; Luke 12:3-9; Acts 4:10-13; Matthew 10:39; Isaiah 51:12-13

Week 16: 1 Thessalonians 5:16-17; 1 Peter 2:19-20; James 1:3-4; Hebrews 6:15; Philippians 4:4

Week 17: 1 Peter 2:9; Ephesians 1:18; Acts 20:32; 2 Corinthians 4:6; Ephesians 5:8

Week 18: 1 John 1:6; Titus 1:16; James 2:14-16; 1 John 4:20

Week 19: 2 Corinthians 3:5-6; Ephesians 2:8-9; 1 Peter 4:12-14; Isaiah 43:2; Romans 6:5

Week 20: Galatians 3:6-14; Romans 4:20-25; Psalm 106:31; Hebrews 11:8

Week 21: Hebrews 12:2-3; James 1:12; Hebrews 10:32; Ephesians 6:11-18; 2 Timothy 2:10

Week 22: Galatians 6:10; James 2:15-16; 2 Corinthians 9:3

Week 23: 1 Corinthians 2:14; Ephesians 4:18-19; Romans 7:22; Hebrews 8:10; John 7:7

Week 24: Deuteronomy 3:22; Deuteronomy 20:4; Joshua 23:3; 2 Chronicles 20:17; Joshua 10:42

Week 25: Romans 12:9; 1 Peter 1:22; Ephesians 4:1-3; 1 Corinthians 13:4-7; Ephesians 4:15

Week 26: John 14:27; 2 Thessalonians 3:16; Isaiah 26:3; Psalm 29:11; Colossians 3:15

Week 27: Psalm 107:20; Mark 1:27; Psalm 33:9; Luke 5:13; Deuteronomy 32:39

Week 28: Romans 8:28-30; 2 Timothy 1:9; 1 Peter 5:10; Ephesians 1:19-21; Romans 8:32

Week 29: Proverbs 21:3; 1 Samuel 15:22; Ecclesiastes 5:1; Jeremiah 22:16; Matthew 5:7

Week 30: Romans 1:16; 2 Corinthians 5:11; 2 Corinthians 11:6; Romans 5:12; Ephesians 4:14

Week 31: Proverbs 16:9; 1 Corinthians 3:7; Proverbs 21:30-31; Psalm 33:16-18; Psalm 121:3-5

Week 32: Philippians 4:8; Luke 21:19; Hebrews 12:1; Romans 12:10; John 15:2

Week 33: Philippians 2:9-11; John 12:23; John 7:39; John 11:4

Week 34: Psalm 121:7; 1 John 5:18; 2 Thessalonians 3:3; Galatians 1:4; Luke 11:4

Week 35: John 17:6-11; Romans 15:18-19; Ephesians 4:11; Acts 4:4

Week 36: Romans 2:4; Habakkuk 2:3; Isaiah 30:18; 1 Timothy 1:16; 2 Peter 3:15

Week 37: Proverbs 16:4; Exodus 9:16; John 19:11; Isaiah 10:15; Daniel 4:34-35

Week 38: Acts Chapter 2; Acts 10:38; Mark 1:12-13; John 1:32; John 3:34

Week 39: The book of Jonah; Luke 11:29-30; Luke 11:32

Week 40: Hebrews 2:1; Proverbs 23:23; Deuteronomy 32:47; Ecclesiastes 7:12; Revelation 12:11

Week 41: John 3:36; James 1:15; John 6:40; Matthew 25:46; John 5:24

Week 42: 2 Corinthians 4:7; Ephesians 2:22; 1 Corinthians 3:16-17; 2 Timothy 3:17; Ephesians 2:10

Week 43: Matthew 5:4; John 14:1; Psalm 147:3; John 16:33; Romans 15:22

Week 44: Nehemiah 9:9; Joshua 24:7; Matthew 14:30-31; 1 John 4:18; Psalm 107:28

Week 45: Isaiah 40:31; Colossians 3:10; Romans 8:18; 1 Peter 5:10; Romans 5:3-5

Week 46: 1 John 5:10; John 9:30; John 5:11

Week 47: Hebrews 13:5; Luke 12:21; Proverbs 16:16; Colossians 3:1-3; 2 Corinthians 4:18

Week 48: 2 Corinthians 4:6; Ephesians 4:22-24; Romans 12:2; Romans 8:29

Week 49: Psalm 33:20; Isaiah 30:18; Genesis 49:18; Isaiah 26:8

Week 50: 1 Timothy 5:6; Romans 12:2

Week 51: 1 Corinthians 1:9; 1 Thessalonians 5:24; 2 Thessalonians 3:3; Titus 1:2; Hebrews 3:6

Week 52: Ephesians 2:8-9; 1 Corinthians 6:11; 2 Timothy 1:9; 1 Peter 3:21; 1 Peter 1:3

A FINAL PRAYER TO THE HOLY SPIRIT

"But the Helper, the Holy Spirit, whom the Father will send in My name, He will teach you all things, and bring to your remembrance all things that I said to you." ~ John 14:26 NKJV

God knows His plans for each and every one of us and reveals to us His plan in His time. Oftentimes we have to experience things to become strong enough to receive and distribute His blessings. So how do we pray for what God has not yet revealed to us? If God is all-knowing, which He is, then the Holy Spirit will know our hearts and pray on our behalf for God's will in our life. Prayers to the Holy Spirit:

- Holy Spirit, I pray that you would guide me in God's will for my life. So much of the world is in me, that I need your help to fuel and strengthen my spirit so that it becomes easier for me to discipline my flesh and keep it under control.

- As I walk this journey in Christ, I know that situations and circumstances will arise that I can't handle alone, and I pray to You for guidance as You know what God's will is for my life. Holy Spirit, you were sent to me as a gift from God because of the sacrifice of Jesus. This sacrifice secured my salvation, and for that I am grateful!

- Holy Spirit, intercede to the Father on my behalf, as I grow in Christ, as I learn to become the person God created me to be, being born again as the scripture says in 2 Corinthians 5:17: *"Therefore, if anyone is in Christ, he is a new creation; old things have passed away; behold, all things have become new"* ~NKJV

- Allow me, Holy Spirit, to sow into the Kingdom with my time, talent, treasure, and devotion, following guidance as God has directed according to His Word in Luke 6:38: *"Give, and it will be given to you; a good measure—pressed down, shaken together, and running over—will be poured into your lap. For with the measure you use, it will be measured back to you."* ~HCSB

And as I become the servant God has created me to be, enter my heart, Holy Spirit, as you advocate on my behalf for all I need to carry out the duties of my purpose in the name of Jesus Christ. I ask this, as the Lord said He would provide in John 14:13-14: *"And whatever you ask in My name, that I will do, that the Father may be glorified in the Son. 14 If you ask anything in My name, I will do it."* ~NKJV

I pray for guidance in my purpose for the Kingdom. I pray so that I may live as God created me to serve in this world. I pray so that God's love will be shown in everything I do. I love you, Lord, and I will keep your commandments as you say in John 14:15.

Amen.

ABOUT THE AUTHOR

Billy Jackson was born in Nashville TN. In his youth he spent his elementary school years in Montgomery, Alabama. He moved back to Nashville and attended the historic Pearl High School his freshman year. His sophomore through senior years Pearl transitioned to Pearl-Cohn High School. Upon graduation from high school, he attended college at another historic institution in Nashville, Fisk University.

Billy is no stranger to serving others. An Army veteran, he served as a crew chief on UH-60 Blackhawk helicopters for seven years. He has also served the Nashville community in law enforcement with the Metropolitan Police Department, now for 21 years. While continuing his service with the government, he has stepped deeper into his calling as a minister of the Gospel and has a deep passion for strengthening marriages one couple at a time.

Billy is married to Yolanda Harris Jackson and together they founded Live In Peace Ministries. They have four beautiful children and three adorable grandchildren. Billy along with Yolanda are fully committed to teaching married couples that life is better together, inspiring them to believe that no matter the how pieces were broken and where they have fallen, they still can live in peace with God. With this hope, they passionately empower married people to live relentlessly as examples of the Gospel for their family, friends, community, and those they encounter along the path God has laid out for them.

www.ingramcontent.com/pod-product-compliance
Lightning Source LLC
Chambersburg PA
CBHW072011290426
44109CB00018B/2203